"A BACKWARD GLANCE
O'ER TRAVEL'D ROADS"

A Reminiscence And A Presentation
Of The Various Forms I Have Employed
Throughout My Long, Long Life

Ah,
Speaking with
A bit of the brogue
Primrose said of
Leonard
(Who was famous for stealing
Bows),
"He might
Stop the show entirely—
Not with his act,

With his bowing."

Jack Foley

"A BACKWARD GLANCE O'ER TRAVEL'D ROADS"

A Reminiscence And A Presentation Of The Various Forms I Have Employed Throughout My Long, Long Life

Jack Foley

Academica Press
Washington~London

Library of Congress Cataloging-in-Publication Data

Names: Foley, Jack (author)
Title: A backward glance o'er travel'd roads : a reminiscence and a
presentation of the various forms i have employed throughout my long,
long life | Jack Foley
Description: Washington : Academica Press, 2021. | Includes references.
Identifiers: LCCN 2020952304 | ISBN 9781680538922 (hardcover) |
9781680538939 (paperback) | 9781680538946 (e-book)

For Sean, Kerry, Sangye
and to the memory of my late wife, Adelle

Contents

I've had it with these cheap sons of bitches who claim to love poetry but never buy a book.

I write poetry to seduce women and to overthrow the Capitalist system. In that order.

REXROTH

FOLEY'S PREDECESSOR, KENNETH REXROTH
drawing by Jack Foley

AUTHOR'S NOTE

In this world of whimsy and wisecracks
In this world of make believe
Life is what you do while waiting
For another dream to leave
         —Jack Foley, Song Lyric

This (scrap)book is a companion volume to my autobiography, *The Light of Evening,* also published by Academica Press. If the latter book is the history of the events of my life with some excursions into the events of my mind, this book is a history of the events of my mind with some excursions into the events of my life. One's spiritual history cannot be separated from the way one encounters the world, but emphases may be different. Nonetheless, there will necessarily be some overlap, and, as Kipling put it in his great poem, "When 'Omer Smote 'Is Bloomin' Lyre," the reader familiar with *The Light of Evening* will find that "old songs turn up again." Poetry arrived in my consciousness in more or less the same way that the words, "Saul, Saul, why dost thou persecute me" arrived in the consciousness of the apostle Paul on the road to Damascus. At the age of fifteen, like most of my friends, I thought of poetry as more or less inconsequential, old-fashioned, dull. A teacher's suggestion that I read Thomas Gray's "Elegy Written in a

Country Churchyard" (1750) changed all that. "The poem seemed to me the most beautiful *sound* I had ever heard. It affected me so deeply that I wanted it to have come out of *me,* not out of Thomas Gray... I understood myself to be a poet." On the face of it, it seemed like an extremely unlikely event. Thomas Gray was an English poet, a letter writer, a Classical scholar, and a professor at Pembroke College, Cambridge. He published only thirteen poems during his lifetime. I was an ambitious Irish-Italian working-class kid who was aware of what the British had done to the Irish. Yet at such life-changing moments, none of that matters. To be a poet meant to change your life. The fifteen-year-old, half-Irish child suddenly transformed himself into an adult, eighteenth-century, British formalist. From there, I began to interrogate the entire history of poetry. The story of my intellectual life is the story of my finding—or trying to find—what Wallace Stevens called "what will suffice." But the history of the mind is not like the history of a tree. It is not a traditional, linear *Bildungsroman.* The mind moves in various directions more or less simultaneously until one suddenly finds oneself in the magic castle on the edge of the sea looking at a mate who is both deeply familiar and completely unknown. If the cowboy usually jumps on the horse and rides further West, the mindboy jumps on the horse and rides off in all the directions that are. It all began with my acceptance of a Facebook challenge issued by a friend, the Japanese poet/artist, Maki Starfield.

CHIQUITA BANANA AND THE LANGUAGE OF VERSE

Anyone of my generation
or a little later
remembers it:
"bananas must be treated
in a special way...
never put bananas
in the refrigerator"
Why?
Because it would take longer
for the bananas to rot:
buy a new banana instead.
It was a lie
not as great a lie
as the cigarette companies produced
when threatened with the truth
but a lie nonetheless
Eventually, we all knew it.
In the sixteenth and seventeenth centuries
a particular language for poetry emerged
Though other modes existed
it was the primary language.
It was flexible, easy to memorize,
could be used
for drama, comedy, epic, almost anything.
It was named for its elements: iambic pentameter, 5 iambs.
It is still in use today
though it is no longer the primary language of poetry.
Prose, with its greater clarity of syntax
and ease of understanding,
did not destroy but greatly diminished it
and the prose-based novel became
the fundamental mode of consciousness.
Free verse is verse adjusted *to prose*
an attempt to keep both verse and prose

in an uneasy balance.
Though formal modes continue,
if there is a current language for verse
free verse is it.
Formal modes continue
especially in the popular songs
to which my poet friends
owe so much allegiance.
When something happens
that makes them happy or sad
they do not go to poetry,
they go to rock 'n' roll,
and this despite the fact that they are poets
learned in the art
and for the most part produce
free verse.
At eighty, looking through my own vast work
and the works of Modernism
I began to see Modernism
as a search for a language
that was neither free verse
nor prose
nor formal modes.
Whitman's word for his work was "song,"
though he did not mean by that
anything genuinely involving music.
Wallace Stevens' "Sunday Morning"
is a magnificent last blast
of iambic pentameter
though of course it also shows up,
often loosely,
in Stevens' later work
and in writers like Robert Frost
and many of the English.
"If only that so many dead lie round,"
wrote Philip Larkin.
But Pound, Joyce,

Eliot in his attempt to find
an equivalent to iambic pentameter
for his theatrical pieces,
Thomas Wolfe in what people have labeled
"singing prose,"
Vallejo in Spanish with Trilce,
so many others, Lorca, Stein, Heidegger,
break with prose
as well as with traditional verse
and produce a language that is—
in the great word of Modernism—
new.
So many look back not to Shakespeare
but to Homer,
to the very beginning of the Western poetic tradition
and attempt to try again.
I listened to all that
and to the lies of the media—
to all the Chiquita Bananas—
and knew
that the language I heard,
the language of everyday,
was not sufficient.
I did not know
what kind of language
was sufficient
and my first poem,
a deep response to Gray's "Elegy,"
was in iambic pentameter.
Looking back at my work as I reach eighty
I realize
that so much of it was this search
for a language,
for what Wallace Stevens called "what will suffice."
The search has produced
a wild collage
of stylistic experiments

which recently I have thought of
as the sounds made
by the severed head of Orpheus.
Eurydice is many things
but she is also
the dazzling language
"the verse that threatens all our prose"
but which has not yet
achieved existence,
verse that remains caught
in the deep underground
of consciousness.
The Waste Land, Ulysses,
Finnegans Wake, The Cantos
are all a mournful cry
to hear her voice
"Yes, I said yes, I will, yes"
but she remains
deep in the ground
deep in the ground
the longed-for,
the language spoken
by the dead.
"They had changed their throats and had the throats of
birds."

#POETMENOTLEAVE PROJECT

"What you really need is an agent."
—Dana Gioia

I have been nominated by my dear friend, Maki Starfield to participate in the poetic marathon #PoetMeNotLeave. During eight days, I will publish three poems a day along with photos.

DAY ONE

"The multiple voices within the mind trajectory
has really gotten me thinking—never formally studied
psychology—but it certainly is an
intriguing explanation for much. And makes the multi
voice poem revolutionary in more than one way...maybe
prophetic as much as
revolutionary."

—Lee Slonimsky on Jack's work as a whole

POEMS WRITTEN BETWEEN THE AGES OF FIFTEEN AND EIGHTEEN

I had come to my hometown, Port Chester, New York, in 1943. When I left in 1958 I understood myself to be a poet. I discovered poetry in 1955, at the age of fifteen. Someone—probably a teacher, perhaps Angela Kelley—suggested that I read Thomas Gray's

18th-Century poem, "Elegy Written in a Country Churchyard." I have no idea why the teacher thought the poem would appeal to me. I thought it very unlikely that I would have much interest in it, but I looked it up in the library and took it home. The poem seemed to me the most beautiful *sound* I had ever heard. It affected me so deeply that I wanted it to have come out of *me*, not out of Thomas Gray, and I immediately sat down and wrote *my own* Gray's "Elegy," in the same stanzaic form and with the same rhyme scheme as the original.

Unlike Gray, I took myself as the subject of my elegy. But its mournful tone—and words like "mem'ries"—was directly traceable to him. I understood the state of mind named in Gray's "Elegy" to be the state of mind of poetry itself; and in reacting so deeply to it, I understood myself to be a poet.

It was by no means a simple state of mind. It had to do with the enormous power of words not merely to reflect but to *create* a "reality," a "mood" which moved me *away* from the daylight world in which I ordinarily functioned and had identity: "I see the *night*...." In some ways Gray's lines hinted at sexuality—surely an issue for me at that time. His flow'r "blushes" and, virginal, "wastes its sweetness on the desert air"; he writes of "the dark, unfathomed *caves*." Speaking the words aloud let me experience them *physically*, with my own breath, coming out of my own body. In *this* situation, mind and body seemed not to be at odds: Thought seemed sensuous, sensuality seemed thoughtful. Self and other were joined here too. Thomas Gray was a long-dead poet of the 18th Century. It was *his* mind that was being expressed in his elegy. Yet his poem seemed to be expressing my own inmost thoughts. It was almost as if Gray's passionate words allowed him to be reincarnated in my body. Further: the fact that Gray's poem took place in a cemetery suggested that my hometown too might be a graveyard, a necropolis—a place I needed to get away from if I wished to live. I don't know whether this thought had occurred to me until that moment, but Gray's poem appeared to ask, "Was I too 'wasting my sweetness on the desert air'"?

There was of course a "real" Thomas Gray, a man who actually existed and who did a number of things beside write poetry. The Gray I was experiencing was not that person but Gray the poet, the bard. Aspects of both our lives seemed suddenly to fall away, to be of little consequence. What did it matter who the man Thomas Gray was? What did it matter who I was—born in New Jersey, growing up in New York? My powerful reaction to Gray's words allowed me to recognize not only who *he* was but who *I* was: *I "was" a poet.* And to "be" a poet meant to be transformed, to move away from the person who lived at 58 Prospect Street and who was 15 years old and who had a mother named Juan and a father named Jack. Poetry offered me another identity, that of the poet; and, in so doing, it offered me another "home"—that of words. The life I led "at home"—"in my house"—was one thing; the life of words was another.

But a person with two homes can be understood as an exile.

Today's photo is my drawing of myself as a baby: early forties.

FIRST POEM, WRITTEN IN 1955 IMMEDIATELY AFTER READING GRAY'S "ELEGY"

I see the night—the restless, eager night
That spreads its shadow softly on the day,
And whispers to the sun's red, burning light
To vanish like a dream and pass away.

I see the night—the darkened mist of night—
And feel the velvet sorrows mem'ries bring;
September's leaves have fallen, old and bright,
And autumn's winds have blown the dust of spring.

I think of days long past, and gone, and dead,
Of all the ancient, withered hopes I've had,
And wonder where the passing hours have fled—
The ghosts of yesterday—forever sad.

O ghosts, my dreams, once breathing, once alive,
Like flower petals in a hurricane,
Were sundered from their stems, no more to thrive,
No more to feel the gentle touch of rain,

No more to hear my reckless, youthful calls,
But banished into bleak eternity,
To come again to me when darkness falls,
As waves upon the seas of memory.

And now the night, with stars and shining lights

All winking, sprightly, like the woodland fawns,
Is fading fast, for with a thousand nights,
There comes the brilliance of a thousand dawns.

*

HIGH SCHOOL YEARBOOK POEM
(1958, written at the request of the Yearbook editor)

VALE

We shall return no more, no more; our days
Have swept aside the dream of endless time
And will return no more. The misty haze
Of autumn will return, and spring—sublime
And simple—will return, and winter's chill,
And summer's sultry shade. (The seasons come
And come again, reflected on the hill
And in the valley, resurrected from
A wind-blown death.) But we shall come no more.
The hills and valley will bleak blackness bring,
And from the shadows emptiness will pour,
And, far behind us, memories will sing.
Alone, we stand in darkness, yet, somewhere,
Our ghosts remain to haunt the silent air.

*

SEQUENCE

a frosted brightness
on the velvet covering
of a dark, dark night

flickers across the fleeting
emptiness of sleeping sky (tanka)

...

the winds blow, biting,
and ice hangs on the tree's bough,
solidly swaying (hokku)

...

a paper flower
fell upon the snow-filled grass—
a touch of scarlet
on the endless white—a rose
of winter, cold, without scent (tanka)

early 1940's
poeta in potentia

DAY TWO

POEMS WRITTEN AT CORNELL UNIVERSITY, WHICH I ENTERED IN 1958, AT THE AGE OF EIGHTEEN

These poems all bring back memories. And all were published in the Cornell literary magazine, *The Trojan Horse*. I recall showing "On the Ultimate Failure of Religiosity"—a poem attempting to deal with my rejection of my childhood faith, Catholicism—to another English major. I wondered what he would make of it. He saw blasphemy but not the death longing—the *liebestod*—which is at the center of the poem. Leaving a religion which promised release from death placed me in the curious position of seeing death as some sort of positive, of having an amorous rather than fearful relationship to it. The birds who eat the bread crumbs make the Hansel and Gretel children impossible to find. "Death" becomes here a sort of secret eroticism—something Catholicism would no doubt have frowned upon. Of course none of this was clear to me at the time of the writing, but I regarded the poem as an important statement, which is why I asked the friend for an *explication de texte,* which I thought he as an English major could supply. In truth, I wasn't certain that anyone would understand it— an uncertainty that remained with me for many years: a sense, born of a fundamental alienation, that my best work would be incomprehensible to others. A recent response to that sense is my assertion that language is not "private" but deeply public; it is always—even in extreme cases of "subjectivity"—leaping beyond itself. "S.T.C." is a poem about Samuel Taylor Coleridge, who often signed his name that way. I remember a friend who loved Coleridge telling me that he rejected the argument the poem presented but was totally taken in by its rhetoric. A print of Utrillo's painting of the Sacré Coeur did indeed hang on the wall of the apartment my wife Adelle and I shared on was it Dryden

Road? My longing for *la vie bohème* had turned into my becoming an English major at an Ivy League university located in a beautiful but cold-in-the winter location on the East Coast. The photograph is from a slightly earlier period: my appearance as part of the Port Chester Senior High School Choir on *The Ed Sullivan Show* (then called *Toast of the Town*): June 6, 1955. I was two months shy of sixteen. I am front row center, with big hair.

ON THE ULTIMATE FAILURE OF RELIGIOSITY

The lineal direction of eternity
is not marked clearly.
Hansel and Gretel-like, I lose my way
and stumble into the wicked house
in the bewildering wood.
I had supposed that death was an accident,
a deviation from the usual path,
yet these sweet-toothed children
munching their gingerbread crumbs
in evident sensuality
are another matter.
The black void inherent in
the fuming kettle
intensifies voluptuousness.
They are content, untrue
to the fairy tale, awaiting
the inevitable movement
to the black pot stirred
by the old hag of the story,
and grateful for the compassionate act
of swift beaks snapping
umbilicus of usual bread.

*

S.T.C.

The astonishing thing about his life
Was not his critical discernment
Or adjustments with his wife
Or with his mistress, learning,
But rather that odd quality
That made him poet, deemphasized
His shortcoming, the tomfoolery
With mystics, and bade him rise,
Stumble, struggle, topple half blindly
Onto Parnassus' top. Oh, to be sure,
He left most of his work undone,
But reading what remains, by turns baffled,
Reproachful, venomous, furious,
Bored,—one finds, when one least expects it,
A curious phrase, an intrusion of wit,
And even from time to time, as clear as icicles,
The fragmentary evidences of genius.

*

THE SACRÉ COEUR ON A WINTER AFTERNOON

Outside, a blizzard's coming into bloom.
The street was like a postcard of the street
an hour ago, but the wind is changing that.
Utrillo's painting of the Sacré Coeur
hangs on the wall—
                    an autumn day,
bright as an apple, with a brilliant sun
beneficently beaming on the dome.

Those archetypes of struggle outside the window
leave us embedded in this single room,
prodigals of fairy tales and visions,
watching, as through a window,
the bohemia of thirty years ago
amble in an autumn afternoon...

The cacophony of wind becomes their chatter,
beaten to a stricter measure,
caught up in the measured afternoon,

and we, the Punch and Judy of our show,
who sat like stumps before the breaking storm,—

we stand before them, dumbly gesturing.

MY APPEARANCE ON *THE ED SULLIVAN SHOW*

There I am at sweet fifteen
On the television screen
Singing in my baritone,
"You Will Never Walk Alone"
As well as that "Beyond the Blue

Horizon" that we had to chew.
When the choir went off pitch
One soprano fixed the hitch
Hitting the exact right note,
Keeping all of us afloat.
Childhood on the TV screen
Flickers at me—there's a scene!
Many of the names have fled
(Many of them now are dead)
But there we all are—lively, noisy,
A thrill for me, born in New Joisey,
A kid my parents (not the stork)
Brought to live in old New York.
Dear Port Chester, Way Back East,
Not the Best, but not the Least.
There I learned to break my tether:
Now I have much better weather.

DAY THREE

MORE POEMS FROM CORNELL UNIVERSITY

Cornell was where I discovered the amazing Paul de Man, whose influence stayed with me throughout my life and whose frequent references to Martin Heidegger brought me to read that life-changing philosopher. I took Robert Durling's excellent course in Dante and read *The Divine Comedy*, the great redeeming, perhaps valedictory poem of Roman Catholicism, and took some rather disappointing courses with the famous professor, M.H. Abrams. Cornell was also where I read *Ulysses* in a course taught by Arthur Mizener, a professor who used to display his Phi Beta Kappa key during class. Mizener's approach was to present *Ulysses* as "the fine novel it really is"—hardly the linguistic approach!—but I had read everything in *The Portable James Joyce* and had a fairly good idea of Joyce's trajectory. I thought *Ulysses*—like all of Joyce's work—wonderful; to this day I cannot recite the marvelous concluding pages of "The Dead" without bursting into tears. A friend, Lewis Rubman, had also given me an LP from the James Joyce Society which featured, among others, Joseph Campbell. The Society played Joyce's incredible recording of the Anna Livia Plurabelle passage from *Finnegans Wake*. I had read that extraordinary passage in the *Portable*, but it was a revelation to hear it in Joyce's Irish tenor. My father's years in vaudeville and much else were in Joyce's imitation of the stage Irishman. It was a marvelous oral performance—an attack on the whole tradition of the novel and, in a way, on the entire English language—and so Homer came to mind. And yet, as Walter J. Ong pointed out, though everything in *Finnegans Wake* cries out to be read aloud, it had to be a book: no one could possibly memorize it. Its language was simultaneously strange and familiar, with constantly multiple meanings. It was in the deepest sense *revelatory*. *Where had that come from*?

When I arrived at Cornell I decided I wanted to understand the whole of English poetry—so I took more courses than I was technically allowed. Even if the professors were dull, as was sometimes the case, the texts were wonderful. I was also a French minor, so I learned about that as well. Things I read in those long-ago years are with me still. I can still recite Pope, still talk about Byron. I remember Carlyle: "Close thy Byron, open thy Goethe."

Today's photograph is my painting of Adelle, watercolor, slightly marred by the years.

UPON LEAVING ATLANTIC CITY (December, 1961)
—written during our honeymoon in "Romantic Atlantic City"

The mother-sea exploded with a roar
before we put the lights out and it vanished.
Not even the ladies marching on the boardwalk
were storm enough to pull us down;
we rode out the daylight, dreaming
of drowsy islands where the water's calm.
Night was our harbor, when the midwife, love,
folded us in with its impossibilities,
fished out our pieces till the game made sense.
Sweetheart, forgive the liars and the fools
who shipped us to this place: they thought it best.
Sleep will bear you into gentler water
where painted characters of kings and castles
glitter like islands, and I will close your ears
to the disarranged palaver of pawns and landlubbers.

*

TUNNEL OF LOVE

Hard-put by the weather,
we await the spring

in sluggish Ithaca.
Stuck
in a ramshackle town,
I love you up to keep the blankets warm.

Back home,
the foghorns bellow in the dingy harbor
while mother putters at her indoor plants.
They are the household deities:
anchored,
they flower in a bad season
while the crazy tugs
teeter and totter in a choppy sea.

Broken by winter,
we huddle mole-like in the covers,

two old sailors
blindly anchored in our Tunnel of Love.

*

This next poem, "Orpheus," was a breakthrough, though it took me
some time to realize exactly where it led me. I was familiar with
the Orpheus story and I had seen Cocteau's film, *Orpheus*, which
had been released in 1950. I had previously written another poem
called "Orpheus" but it was not, as Eliot and Pound used to say,
"of the first intensity." I decided to see whether I might have
another try at it, to see whether a revision might make it better. As
I was typing the opening lines of the first "Orpheus" poem,
something happened to me. I was suddenly possessed by another

poem, also called "Orpheus" and using the opening lines I had typed. But I had absolutely no idea where this poem was taking me. It was simply enormously insistent and I had no choice but to stay with it until it was finished. It was a totally ecstatic experience. I had no idea where the poem had come from and practically no idea what it was about, though the Orpheus myth seemed to be relevant to it. The poem was indeed a breakthrough—Pound's "Mauberley" was undoubtedly an influence along with Cocteau—though it took me some time to find out what exactly it "was." People liked the poem, and it was eventually published in *The Beloit Poetry Review*, though I have never published it in any of my books.

Despite the intensity of its initial appearance—or perhaps *because* of the intensity of its initial appearance—I lost touch with the poem. Part of the problem was that I really didn't know what to do with this breakthrough, didn't know where I might go with it. In addition, I felt that there was an embarrassingly homophobic moment in it, an attack on Walt Whitman of all people—and this despite the fact that a moment later in the poem I am praising and lamenting the equally gay Garcia Lorca. In any case, the poem was not alive for me for many, many years. I recited it publicly only once, at Cornell, when I was 21. A recent radio show was the second time I publicly recited the poem. But, amazingly, it came back with an incredible intensity. Sixty years later, I felt its power again, just as I had felt it when I was at Cornell. Whatever had blocked it over all those years was now gone. Sixty years just melted away as I spoke those words, this "story."

ORPHEUS

1.
I have a story to tell you, lady, some
old lie about a poet. You
will not believe it.
                              We sit here waiting
for something extraordinary to happen,
something to blast us out of the polite
restrictions of a proper conversation,
something big. I have a story, lady,
that will raise your hair,
a calculated bomb to blow you up.
                                    Listen:

Orpheus charmed trees
and the waves of the sea
with his improbable melodies

                    (being Greek, his profile
                    was extraordinarily handsome)

2.
(Chanson Blanche D'Orphée)

On this hill, lady,
I play my lute,
enchanting birds
till they sit stock still
while ants
dance

and my words move mountains.

(Chanson Noire D'Orphée)

The cave is dark
and hot as hell.
My baby's there,
there on a slab in this god-forsaken place

      I sing, then, sing
      out of the bitter fury of my veins.

3.
Walt Whitman walks on the harbor, watching
seagulls scatter, his beard full of lice.
There he goes with his body electric,
chanting his chansons in the morning,
                never shaving.

Walt eyes the sailors, with *their* bodies electric,
electric to him, Walt Whitman,
chanting his chants in the morning,
                never shaving.

      4.
      Garcia Lorca chants Walt Whitman—
      Orpheus in the saddle,
      his beautiful eyes are gleaming.
      Never will there be an Andalusian
      as handsome as he.

      Now the worms eat him,
      now the worms chew up Garcia Lorca

      shot in the head for political reasons.

5.
I don't understand this at all.
    Think of Tennyson,
of Longfellow.
    They were poets.

Why must you be so unpleasant?

6.
Consider Orpheus, then:
old & bald & lonely
(with an eye for the ladies)

he goes on singing, singing
in a city run down by barbarians

        (on the high & honeying hill
        the lovers—)

DAY FOUR

MORE FROM CORNELL

My friend Warren Wechsler and I decided to write a musical. The choice was Henry Fielding's novel, *Tom Jones*. Warren wrote the music, I wrote the lyrics and did a tap dance to open the second act. My father had been a tap dancer in vaudeville and I knew enough of the art to work out a routine for myself and a partner.

Mike Abrams, scion of Abrams Art Books and a BMOC ("Big Man On Campus"), wrote a serviceable first act but failed to write a second. Somewhat desperate, Warren and I enlisted the aid of Stephen Sahlein, who rather nervously wrote a somewhat wordy second act. I didn't read Fielding's novel but worked with the script Abrams and Sahlein had provided. Our director, Bryn Matthews, came from Ithaca College. Warren feared that the reviews would say, "Good Fielding, No Hit," but in fact the two reviews we received were both quite favorable. One tended to favor the show's music; the other tended to favor the show's lyrics. We were even asked to repeat the show at a weekend to which Cornell parents were invited.

The plot in brief: Master Blifil wishes to marry Miss Sophia Western in order to gain control of the estate she will inherit upon the death of her father, Squire Western. Unfortunately, Sophia does not care for him but loves Tom Jones, a servant boy on the estate. Lady Bellaston, Blifil's ally who also loves Jones, convinces Blifil that the only way he can marry Sophia is to rape her: then he will *have* to marry her. Blifil is reluctant to do this for various reasons. There were pages of rather dull dialogue indicating all this. I turned them all into a song. *The Fantasticks*—a 1960 musical I had seen in its original production—had a comic song about rape; I decided to write one for *Tom Jones*. Blifil is of course completely unsuccessful in his attempt; no one for an instant believes that his threat is real. I was obviously thinking of Gilbert & Sullivan, but I knew I was dealing with a subject G&S would never have dealt with—so the song seemed rather edgy. It inevitably brought down the house at the time we put on the play, but I'm not sure we could even perform it nowadays, when the threat of rape is generally regarded with a justified seriousness that is nowhere in the song.

I should remark here that my interest in the "deep" art of poetry in no way annihilated my interest in the "light" art of musical comedy. I greatly admired the art of lyricists such as Lorenz Hart, Ira Gershwin, Cole Porter. Porter—the coiner of the word "tinpantithesis"—was a particular favorite: "Manhattan, / I'm up a tree. / The one that I adored / Is bored / With me." I obtained a book of Porter's lyrics from the library and learned much about rhyme and its uses—to say nothing of Porter's marvelous wit. He was alive during my childhood and sometimes appeared on television—a medium in which I saw the marvelous Noël Coward-Mary Martin "special," *Together With Music*, and experienced English Music Hall at its finest. The sound of Coward's amazing speech (created, I understand, because of his deaf parents) and songs like "Uncle Harry's Not a Missionary Now" stayed with me forever. I felt that even Shakespeare, whose plays often featured music, was in a way the author of musical comedies. The form could move easily between "low" elements and "high" elements and still remain intact. Very liberating.

THE RAPE SONG

LADY BELLASTON:

Master Blifil, stop your sniffling
And listen to my plan
I would offer you a chance to be
A most heroic man
With a single little action
You'd be cheered with loud hurrah:
Your fame would be eternal
If you'd *rape* Miss Sophia.

TOGETHER, BLIFIL SHOCKED:

If you'd rape (If I'd rape!)
If you'd rape (If I'd rape!)
If you'd rape (If I'd rape!) Miss Sophia!

BLIFIL:

Lady Bellaston, I hardly am
The sort of man you wish
For though others like to swagger
I would much prefer to swish
I'd endure a small seduction
That's a minor sort of scrape
But I'm surely not the man
For the vicissitude of rape

TOGETHER:

The viciss-
The viciss-
The vicissitude of rape.

LADY BELLASTON: If you'd rape

BLIFIL: (insulted) If I'd rape!
LADY BELLASTON: If you'd rape
BLIFIL: If I'd rape!
And the consequences I could not escape!
LADY BELLASTON: If you'd try
BLIFIL: (unmoved) If I'd try
LADY BELLASTON: If you'd try
BLIFIL: (scornfully) If I'd try
LADY BELLASTON: You would soon be living high
BLIFIL: Not I!

BLIFIL:

Lady Bellaston, I wish that you'd
Be gentle, sweet and kind
I'd be happier if you could be
A little more refined!
There's a tempest in my teapot
There's a ruffle in my cape
But I hardly am the man
For the indignity of rape

TOGETHER:

The indig
The indig
The indignity of rape

LADY BELLASTON: If you'd rape
BLIFIL: If I'd rape
LADY BELLASTON: If you'd rape
BLIFIL: If I'd rape!
LADY BELLASTON: And the consequences you would soon escape.
If you'd *try*
BLIFIL: If I'd try
LADY BELLASTON: If you'd try

BLIFIL: (suddenly considering it) If I'd *try…*
LADY BELLASTON: You would soon be *living high*
BLIFIL: But I—

LADY BELLASTON:

AND apart from the attractions
Of the urge to procreate
When you're married to Miss Sophia
You're *wed to the estate*
Master Jones would be your servant,
Squire Western your papá…

(pause)

BLIFIL (thoughtfully):

I have come to a decision:
I will rape Miss Sophia!

TOGETHER (triumphantly):

I will rape (He will rape)
I will rape (He will rape)
I (He) will rape Miss Sop-hi-a!

"The Lobster's Testimony" was the last poem I wrote at Cornell. I remember reading it to the famous professor, M.H. Abrams (no relation to my friend Mike). Abrams kindly praised it. Though Paul de Man had more effect on me than anyone else at Cornell, I never read him any of my poetry. Criticism and poetry remained separate activities. In fact, in many subtle ways I was encouraged to write criticism rather than poetry at Cornell, and I discovered that I was good at writing criticism. Like most college programs, Cornell's English Department tended to produce people who felt comfortable with analysis but uncomfortable with emotion—particularly with personal emotion. Besides, I could use criticism to defend my sometimes "obscure" poetry.

The next poem, "The Lobster's Testimony," was a response to "Pot Aux Foux," Daniel G. Hoffman's wonderful poem about Gérard de Nerval. Hoffman's poem referred to French literature—my minor—and was somewhat reminiscent of the work of John Crowe Ransom, which I admired. It had been published in a book I had liked and had even reviewed for *The Trojan Horse: A Little Geste and Other Poems* (1959). Years later, I came into contact with Hoffman and sent him the poem. It began a correspondence. Apart from my very first poem, "The Lobster's Testimony" was my first conscious effort of *responding* to a poem another poet had written. This impulse later became a practice I called "writing"—as opposed to reading—"between the lines," one of the many ways in which I insisted that the impulse behind a poem was "multiple" rather than "individual," one of the many ways I moved against the lyrical ego.

POT AUX FOUX

Gérard de Nerval's ribbon led
A large live lobster. Men, like geese

At their communion hissed, or fled,
Made hue, and cried, 'Breach of the peace!'

Enjoined by irate hierarch
He pled *non vult contendere*
'Because,' he said, 'it does not bark
And knows the secrets of the sea.'

Gérard they packed to Dr. Blanche
(Cold-water cures in a year, or less);
The lobster, after that dimanche
When Gendarme's wife served bouillabaisse,

Lost interest in philosophy.
Now Nerval's hung himself, who'll heed
The lucubrations of the sea?
The tides, in bowls, resound, recede.
        —Daniel G. Hoffman

THE LOBSTER'S TESTIMONY

Not even Dr. Blanche could tell
and poor Nerval would not confess:
instead of making bouillabaisse
he tied a ribbon to my shell.
(He did it for the sake of art.)

Alas! How could the bourgeoisie
have understood the sea or me:
they sent him packing to Montmartre!
And I,—the concierge was chosen
to serve me up as lobster stew:
while I turned red, Nerval turned blue.

Dead, dead as a fish and flesh quick-frozen,
they found him hanging presently—

le bon Gérard, unmindful of
the calefaction of my love
among the secrets of the sea.

Today's photo: Jack and Adelle in costume for *Tom Jones*.

DAY FIVE

In 1963 Adelle and I were heading west, on our way to Berkeley, California. I had been awarded a Woodrow Wilson Fellowship; Adelle was soon to find a job at the Federal Reserve Bank of San Francisco. Paul de Man good-naturedly told me that I had better get my tennis game together because that's all anyone did in Berkeley. In 1962 I had finally learned to drive. We purchased a 1956 Oldsmobile to make the trip across country. We found an apartment without much trouble. The following year we found a place in Oakland; ten years later we bought a house in Oakland. I'm still living in that house.

In Berkeley my writing stopped almost entirely as I concentrated on graduate school or participated in that explosion of energy we call "the sixties." A friend, Lewis Rubman, knew many of the people involved with The Free Speech Movement, and so I got to meet them early on. I protested the war and experimented with LSD and marijuana. (I deliberately took acid *before* I took marijuana so that no one could accuse me of "going on to the harder stuff.") I learned rock songs and played them on my electric guitar. Until that time my guitar playing had depended entirely on sheet music. I now learned to trust (and develop) my ear. Berkeley radio station KPFA broadcast an astonishing range of art programming, which I found fascinating. I first heard Gertrude Stein's voice on KPFA, through the good offices of Charles Amirkhanian. Stein read "If I Told Him: A Completed Portrait of Picasso." I was delighted to discover that I loved the piece—and understood it! I immediately began to acquire Stein's books.

I had hoped that Cornell would provide me with an intellectual community. It did not. My experience at Berkeley was similar, though again there were moments of excitement. Josephine Miles, Joseph Kramer, Paul Alpers, Stanley Fish and others taught courses which interested me. Henry Nash Smith's course included Charles Feidelson, Jr.'s excellent book, *Symbolism And American*

Literature, with its stimulating discussions of Melville, Poe and Whitman. A 1971 class taught by James Breslin introduced me to many writers whom I had previously neglected, particularly to William Carlos Williams, whose masterly *Spring and All* was on the reading list. We also read Robert Duncan's magnificent *Bending the Bow*. (I had bought Duncan's *Selected Poems* in Ithaca and been fascinated by "The Venice Poem" and the seldom anthologized "Homage to the Brothers Grimm.") Born in Oakland, California, Duncan lived in San Francisco and often gave lectures and readings. I saw him frequently in Berkeley going to the bookstores or the library and attended his readings. He was always a gorgeous, eye-catching figure as he moved through the world. He attended a reading given by his friend David Bromige and swept into the room wearing his customary cape. I was entranced. There were also poets in Breslin's class: Ron Silliman, David Melnick, and Rochelle Nameroff had all recently published books through a press called "Ithaca House," located, ironically enough, at Cornell University. Paul Lobo Portugés was also taking the class. In addition, James Breslin was the judge of Berkeley's Yang Poetry Prize that year, and a little selection of my poems was one of the winners. Ron Silliman received first prize. Still, I could hardly call myself a writer. By 1970 I was really nothing more than a professional graduate student.

FIRST POEM WRITTEN ON REACHING BERKELEY, CALIFORNIA, 1963:

Yes, yes it is

the West.

I remembered that as Adelle and I drove across country I noticed that, as the day began to end, the sun was always in my eyes. "Of course it is," said Adelle. "We're driving West."

The story of my early time at Berkeley is the story of my growing increasingly dissatisfied with my presence in academics. There was much that I disliked about what I was doing, but I had no plausible substitute. My desire to get out of my life became stronger and stronger, and I began to project that desire onto my relationship with Adelle. The result was that we separated for a short time. I moved out of the house and found a small room. I also hunted up a job. I worked for Ed Landberg at the Cinema Guild in Berkeley. My technical title was "manager," but in fact I was really little other than a slightly glorified ticket taker. Other duties included looking for Pauline Kael's notes on films Landberg was showing and "walking the ladder" to change the names on the marquee. I remember one night when I had to remain in the ticket booth while people inside the theater were laughing and enjoying the film, probably an American comedy from the 30s or 40s. Feeling sorry for myself, I wrote a poem that was partly John Skelton (I enjoyed "Skeltonics"), partly John Crowe Ransom (whom I had heard read at Cornell), partly Wallace Stevens, and perhaps partly Cole Porter. Some friends had been giving me a hard time about my gaining weight. The speaker of my poem has lost so much weight that he has made himself into a skeleton.

THE SKELETON'S DEFENSE OF CARNALITY

Truly I have lost weight, I *have*
lost weight,
grown lean in love's defense,
in love's defense grown grave.
It was concupiscence
that brought me to the state:
all bone and a bit of skin
to keep the bone within.

Flesh is no heavy burden
for one possessed of little
and accustomed to its loss.
I lean to love, which leaves me lean
till lean turn into lack.

A wanton bone, I sing my song
and travel where the bone is blown
and extricate true love from lust
as any man of wisdom must.

Then wherefore should I rage
against this pilgrimage
from gravel unto gravel?
Circuitous I travel
from love to lack
and lack to lack,
from lean to lack

and back.

My desire to *fous-moi le camp* also found expression in a poem I tacked onto a long paper I wrote on William Blake's poem, "Holy Thursday"—the "Holy Thursday" from *Songs of Innocence*:

'Twas on a Holy Thursday, their innocent faces clean,
The children walking two and two, in red and blue and green,
Grey headed beadles walk'd before, with wands as white as snow,
Till into the high dome of Pauls they like Thames' waters flow.

Oh what a multitude they seem'd, these flowers of London town!
Seated in companies they sit with radiance all their own.
The hum of multitudes was there, but multitudes of lambs,
Thousands of little boys and girls raising their innocent hands.

Now like a mighty wind they raise to heaven the voice of song,
Or like harmonious thunderings the seats of Heaven among.
Beneath them sit the aged men, wise guardians of the poor;
Then cherish pity, lest you drive an angel from your door.

My paper was a wild, ecstatic mixture of things including genuine analysis, readings in Blake's sources—I remember finding considerable significance in the fact that it wasn't physically possible for anyone, including children, to walk into "the high dome of Pauls"—and my half-acknowledged desire to get out of the academy. I was incensed that Blake's critics didn't allow for his linguistic skill—didn't know for example that "blake" was an old form of "black" and that this had some relevance to "The Little Black Boy": "And I am BLAKE but oh, my soul is white." The paper ended with a never-published poem that combined leaving Adelle with leaving academics. My paper called it "a poem of gentle wrath." I was aware as I wrote it that the word "verse" meant "a turning." The "bow" is a rainbow.

CONTRA ACADEMICUM, GENTILLIES

She whispered, saying *Love*
and so I loved
and layed a lovely time
She laughed and said *I do*
and so I did
and did she too
She said *O heartless one, O wretch*
because I strayed away a stretch
because I would not stay

I hung my hark upon a limb
I would not listen to her whim
I rumbled like a cloud and roared
For forty nights I poured and poured
Until she said *Re-turn*
And so I did and made a 'bow
And layed her high and layed her low
And left her then (a lass!)

She said *Come back* but I said *No*

I left her weeping on the grass
And softly said *ado, adoo*
For who can join a Jill and Jack?

I turned and saw:
And told the bundle on my back,
There will be other loves to lack

The Holy Thursday passage was again a poem responding to a poem, even a kind of "translation," the insertion of myself into someone else's poem and the creation of a hybrid poem, a "multiple" poem in which two voices spoke. One was the voice that read the poem; one was the voice that responded to the poem:

WE HAVE HERE—AS WE HAVE AT THE CONCLUSION OF "THE ECHOING GREEN"—A KIND OF GRADUAL FADING OF THE LIGHT IN WHICH THINGS ARE NO LONGER SEEN CLEARLY AND IN WHICH THE SOUNDS WE "HEAR" TEND TO BECOME SOMEWHAT DISTANT: "ALL THE HILLS ECHOED." AT THIS POINT, I THINK, LANGUAGE BECOMES SOMETHING CLOSE TO PURE POTENTIALITY, TO PURE "SOUND" OR "MUSIC," TO THE "SONG" THAT THE PIPER PIPES. WHAT BLAKE IS ATTEMPTING TO MAKE US DO, I SUSPECT, IS TO TREAT *ALL* OF HIS WORDS IN THE SAME WAY THAT WE MUST TREAT THE NAMES OF HIS CHARACTERS: WE MUST CONTINUALLY RECOMBINE THEM, MUST TURN THEM AROUND AND AROUND IN OUR MINDS UNTIL THEY BECOME WORDS WHICH, THOUGH DIFFERENT, INVOLVING OTHER LETTERS, RETAIN IN THEIR SOUNDS THE ECHOES OF

ONE ANOTHER. BLAKE HIMSELF USED WORDS OF THE
BIBLE IN ORDER TO CREATE NEW HARMONIES,
HARMONIES WHICH "CHIMED" WITH THOSE OF THE
BIBLE, AND I THINK "HOLY THURSDAY" WAS MEANT TO
SERVE THE SAME PURPOSE. TWAS ON A, FOR EXAMPLE,
MIGHT EASILY BECOME TWAS HONOR, HOSANNA; THE
SEATS OF HEAVEN, THE SAINTS OF HEAVEN, THE SEEDS
OF HEAVEN; BENEATH THEM SIT, BE NEATH THEM
SAID; WHITE AS SNOW, WHY 'TIS SNOW, WHY 'TIS NOW;
TILL INTO, TELL UNTO, TOLL UNTO; THE VOICE OF
SONG, THEY VOICE HIS SONG, THEIR VOICE IS SONG,
THEIR VOICE, HIS SONG; THE FLOWERS OF LONDON
TOWN, OR LAND ATONED, OR LENTEN TIME; BUT
MULTITUDES OF LAMBS, BUT MULTITUDES OF LANDS,
BUT MULTITUDES OF LIMBS, BOUGHT MULTITUDES OF
LAMBS; THOUSANDS OF LITTLE BOYS, THOSE SANDS OF
LITTLE BOYS; O WHAT A, O WATER; THE HUM OF
MULTITUDES, THE HOME OF MULTITUDES, THE HYMN,
THE HAM, THE HIM OF MULTITUDES; THEY LIKE
THAMES WATERS FLOW, THEY LIGHT TIME'S WATERS
FLOW, THEIR NIGHTTIMES WATERS FLOW; RADIANCE
ALL THEIR OWN, RADIANCE ALL THEREROUND,
RADIANCE ALL THEREON, REGENTS ARE THERE
CROWNED; THE CHILDREN WALKING, THE CAULDRON
WAKING, THE CALLED ARE WALKING; HARMONIOUS

THUNDERINGS, OUR MOAN, HIS THUNDERINGS; THE VOICE, THE VOWS, THE JOYS.

Oddly enough, the notion of turning words around and around in our minds was one of the things that led me to the perception that the opening lines of Yeats' poem, "The Second Coming," were not an image of chaos but an image of escape. Paul de Man's brilliant view of Yeats stayed with me then and now. Today's photo is my drawing of Robert Duncan.

DAY SIX

Under the influence of James Breslin's course and its participants I began to produce a kind of experimental verse. Remembering both Paul Valéry—whose work I had read in Paul de Man's class—and a brand of candy, I put these poems together in a short sequence called "Charmes." Each of the poems was an ecstatic, only partially understood experience, though there was a tendency throughout for the poems to center in a word which was both a noun and a verb. I was aware of Ernest Fenollosa's *The Chinese Written Character As a Medium for Poetry*:

"A true noun, an isolated thing, does not exist in nature. Things are only the terminal points, or rather the meeting points of actions, cross sections cut through actions, snap-shots. Neither can a pure verb, an abstract motion, be possible in nature. The eye sees noun and verb as one...Like nature, the Chinese words are alive and plastic, because *thing* and *action* are not formally separated."

I associated the appearance of these noun/verbs with a release from some of the tensions that were constantly present in my consciousness.

Here is the third:

randy belly   .   look & come   .   there are clouds in the—

                                   .

                    hardly the ice   .   ends

                                   .

folding   lines

quiet is the

.

cross-ing the
    crossing   toss-

crossed

And the eleventh, which quotes both Keats and Dylan Thomas
("the strut and trade of *charms*") and plays on a vulgar word for
my Italian heritage:

DARKLING NOW THE DAY GOES . . .

strut & trade   who relegate!

   -here!- with another page of m

    anuscript   to add to .

Such poems were wonderful when they came, but they were few
and far between. Though the poems seemed to celebrate my
entrance into the ecstatic state in which poetry was possible
("cross-ing the / crossing   toss- / crossed"), I had no idea how that
state might be induced or how in fact I had fallen into it.

Another poem from this period of uncertainty arose out of my reading Milton's great *Paradise Lost* (Stanley Fish's class) and my lifelong obsession with leaves—an obsession that goes back to Thomas Wolfe and Shelley's "Ode to the West Wind," to say nothing of Whitman's "leaves of grass" and Homer's "the generations of men are like the generations of leaves." I understood but did not quite formulate the notion that words constantly leap beyond themselves just as leaves fall. The speaker of my poem is a leaf, and I was aware that "superfluous" is by etymology "overflowing." Milton's highly Latinate English and his play upon etymologies were very much on my mind in all of this. "Inextricate" is my coinage.

FALL

Break then
Plummet—
Crack!
I fell
crashing into Vallombrosa—caught!—
but not by Milton's simile
and not for naught

      Limbless and forlorn
      I had no love to give
      nor any purgative
      So let the born be borne:
      I vanished in a bog

           Dolor, doloris

singing thus
it was not less calamitous
it was not less that leaf and leaf
mourned that I should come to grief
Upon this doleful bog
I fell amuck agog
repeating leaf by leaf
the paradigm of Grief

—No, no: mendacities!
These dead leaves tell no tale
All lamentation done
one is not anyone:
a thunderclap and off!

2

Here where the leaves lie thick
thus sang my elegy
and trembled to the quick
To what finality?

Inextricate so long,
I lingered in the wind

Before I turned to dust
I drifted (ah!)
Superfluous

The poem's shape suggests the arc of a leaf's falling, and it has elements not only of Milton but of the playfulness and interest in Latinate English of John Crowe Ransom. It too was an ecstatic experience and was by no means fully understood. The leaf not only falls: it *drops out.*

By 1974 I had finally had enough of graduate school. I made a last-ditch effort to write a PhD thesis. A long paper on Shakespeare's *Cymbeline*, written for Joseph Kramer's class, might have been the basis of a thesis. The only problem was that the paper didn't mention a single critic. I set about to remedy that. The books I needed were sometimes taken out of the main library. In the undergraduate library, however, there was a set of stacks which had just about everything. Nobody ever touched it. Unfortunately, as I read the critics I found myself getting angry. *Cymbeline* was not a play which anyone seemed to have understood very well. Even people whose work I usually liked had little of interest to say about it. What had been lost in the case of this play was the historical knowledge—common in Shakespeare's day—that Cymbeline's reign coincided with the birth of Christ. The characters in *Cymbeline* have no knowledge of Christ's birth—they are Pagans; nonetheless as the play progresses they begin to act like Christians. Finally, I got up and wandered over to the modern poetry section. There I came upon Charles Olson's *Maximus IV V VI*. I found the book amazing. I'm not sure I understood it in the usual sense in which one "understands" things. On the other hand, I understood it. *Maximus IV V VI*, with its size, its ample white space, its *freedom* was a revelation, or, as Jake Berry said about another book, a baptism. I went back and forth between the critics and Olson until I realized that I was in fact acting out a little psychodrama. Do you want to be *this* or do you want to be *this*? The decision was obvious. I left school. I wanted to be Olson.

Leaving school freed me towards reading again. I plunged into Gertrude Stein and Pound's *Cantos*. Like Robert Kelly as he tells it in *A Controversy of Poets*, I felt transformed by Williams' "astonishing" "Asphodel That Greeny Flower." I read the Beats with better understanding than ever before. L=A=N=G=U=A=G=E poets were just beginning to publish, and I was aware of their work. A KPFA program introduced me to Kerouac's marvelous reading style. I read all the Duncan I could find. Michael McClure's essay, "Phi Upsilon Kappa," opened his work to me ("Writing this is a kind of pain as well as a joy at the chance to make a new liberty"). KPFA broadcast an amazing production of Artaud's radio play *Pour En Finir Avec Le Jugement De Dieu* which included Artaud himself. I immediately hunted up *The Theater and Its Double*. I also read Louis Zukofsky, Jack Spicer, Larry Eigner, H.D., Amiri Baraka, Clayton Eshleman, Ishmael Reed, and Adrienne Rich. Through Rich I came upon Judy Grahn's stunning poem, *A Woman Is Talking To Death* and then her later poetry and her wonderful essays. Walter J. Ong's work became an endless source of inspiration and insight. Gregory Bateson taught me a good deal, as did Carl Sauer. I explored the occult: A.E. Waite, Crowley, Max Heindel, Corinne Heline. (Her little book on the moon in occult lore is masterly. Jake Berry is the only person I ever met who had heard of her and, indeed, had a copy of her work.) I finally read Heidegger (to whom Paul de Man was always referring) as well as Wittgenstein, Gurdjieff, Whitehead, Freud, Jung and Foucault. Hannah Arendt's *The Human Condition* was read and re-read. Her relationship to Heidegger was fascinating.

Partly through the good offices of Charles Amirkhanian at KPFA, I was listening to experimental music as well as reading experimental poetry. Charles Ives' *Concord Sonata* and his book, *Essays Before A Sonata* were enormous influences, as were his songs. I first heard Lou Harrison on KPFA and was able to attend several of his concerts at near-by Mills College. I had acquired Kenneth Rexroth's wonderful edition of D.H. Lawrence's poetry in Ithaca. Now I was reading Rexroth, who had a show on KPFA. My friend Ed Michel gave me a collection of records he had produced, so I began to listen seriously to jazz. Eisenstein's essays were tremendously exciting, as was Abel Gance's marvelous "polyvision" film, *Napoleon*, which Adelle and I saw at The Avenue Theater in San Francisco. I haunted UC Berkeley's Pacific Film Archive and published a few essays on film, particularly on Alfred Hitchcock. Hitchcock's transformation of a pre-existing text—something he did not write—into film was not unlike my transformation of something I did not write into a "hybrid" poem. Both these transformations suggested the practice of collage—its transformation of pre-existing materials—and the jazz musician's transformation of a pre-existing tune. At the heart of all these transformations is history, the fact of time, and the mysterious yet liberating presence in us of "others." I began to think seriously about the art of painting. Clyfford Still's work fascinated me. A 1977 exhibition of Jess's work at the UC Berkeley University Art Museum had an enormous impact. I discovered Max Ernst, Kandinsky's paintings and his marvelous book, *Concerning the Spiritual in Art*. Etc.

Thought was once again an adventure, not a chore. There were no "assignments," only the constant possibility of learning something new.

Today's photo is my drawing of Charles Olson.

archeologist of morning —

DAY SEVEN

Not self-expression: discovery.

On June 25, 1974 I was utterly depressed about my writing. I had

just brought our car in for servicing—never a happy obligation—

and taken the bus back home. I was extremely tired and believed at that moment I would never produce anything of any value. Glancing at a collection of Olson's essays—particularly at "Human Universe"—I noticed a sentence which began, "If there is any truth at all to the idea that...." Certain that nothing would come of it, I typed on a piece of paper, "If there is any truth at all" and added, as if in commentary, "(there is)." I went on to appropriate others of Olson's phrases, changing them if I felt like it. (Olson actually wrote, "It is *not* the Greeks I blame.")

> if there is any truth at all (there is)
> it is the greeks I blame
> the lines in which
>   speech takes place
> & Melville did....

Next I took a recent passage from my journal,

> a waking dream.
> Someone (me, not me) on a rooftop. Being chased?
>   Crowds. The man's friends below, holding a
> net which looks like an awning, urge him.
>   Tremendous distance!
> The man jumps!—he misses the awning.
> I remark (it is remarked to me): he didn't check
>   which way the wind was blowing,

and retyped it, moving my fingers slightly so I would hit some of the wrong keys and leaving out some of it, revising as I went along:

a wajubg dreanL
sineibe OOne.bitg neOOib a riiftioOObeubg cgased.
Criwds the man's friends bekiw
gikdubg a bet kiijs kuje ab wawbubg greeb
            tremendous distance
yrge
   urge him

   to killowatts

My depression vanished. The poem suddenly came alive. Its seemingly obvious discovery that literature was made out of *letters* was extraordinarily liberating, and its concluding lines, only half-understood when I wrote them, "the page is not the / natural dividing point," thrust me into an entirely new direction. A sequence of such poems followed. I called it "Letters" and dedicated it to "the sixth Marx brother: Typo." (Olson's praise of the typewriter in his famous essay, "Projective Verse," was undoubtedly in the back of my mind.) I of course knew that much of the poem was nonsense, but I liked the effect of sense emerging from nonsense, of words suddenly appearing (or almost appearing) out of the random accumulation of letters. ("The urge to kill" becomes here "the urge to killowatts"—depression and violence turning into energy: "the rain jumps / the man jumps.") I also liked the sense these poems gave me of a foreign language which I ALMOST understood. They were like a message from another world—something one might work at decoding, something that pushed one's understanding forward even if it was ultimately frustrated. The poem was not an area of self expression but an area of discovery and even healing: "the / dawn in a period when no dawn is possible," followed by a play on the primary colors of light: "rare [for red]   blue   and green unknown." I was also attentive to sound, though I realized that many of the "words" were virtually unpronounceable. Later, when I wrote "choruses" to be performed by Adelle and me, it was a question of various phrases and lines appearing out of the cacophony of two voices speaking simultaneously. People sometimes complained that the two voices got in each other's way, they couldn't understand what was said. They didn't understand that that was part of my intention. The notion that poetry existed, like prose, to communicate a paraphrasable "message" was not uppermost in these pieces. The sense that the mind was a cacophony of voices was. I thought of these pieces not as collage but as collision texts. Here are the two opening poems from "Letters." I was aware that the first line of the first poem (like the concluding line of Olson's *Maximus* poems!) was a line of strict iambic pentameter.

if there is any truth at all (there is)
it is the greeks I blame
the lines in which
                    speech takes place
& Melville did
                    no chance to take away
does not change

             the sun was done with her
and the meeting-edge, the
               off-shoot culture
    a place called Pueblo
noting what you have noted
            bone muscle nerve brain blood
definition & expression of it
           reindeer language permits
    in his last poem
to the women who are buried in England

      a wajubq dreanL
   sineibe Oone.bit neOOib a riiftioOObeubg cgased.
    Criwds   the man's friends bekiw
     gikdubg a bet kiijs kuje ab wawbubg 'greeb
           tremendous distance
yrge
   urge him

       to killowatts

it is not done yet
          figure on this (as so many things)

the rain jumps
the man jumps

historic fiction with a bearing
           in Latin lettering
the story contains
        any account of
naturally divides itself
       the
dawn in a period when no dawn is possible

rare   blue   and green unknown

───────────────────────────

the page is not the

           natural dividing point

2

thr gsbot bivyim yhr derryinhd yhr nounfsty
yhr dvugg
yo slloe yhr dprvisllplainted grass bag
refuse to divulge
yhr eoetlf ot yr nrst nr vsllrf yo sloe yhr dpitiyd yhodr mrfis
I eill trvkon him
yhr rdyrrm in ehivh nre yrttioyyt
ehivh oyhrtd msy ginf yoo Vhtidyisn
the likelihood that the village
you ertr s punliv return had no connection sll in bsin
motr onr yhsn snoyhrt brty yhivk zz & Isthr
we talked of a part of the craving the fullest satisfact ion
errk dytryvh
I hsbr likrnrf you yhr noyr og s honh   *when he kills*
in new territory
in domr indysnvrd yhr nrst id pryiyionrf
      fur yo hhr dhspinh hsnf & yhr philodophivsl minf
to allow the spirits
iy id ptimstily sd s vtiyiv eiyh Johndon I quarrle
plrsde etiyr.   Snf iy eill trsvh mr.
Yhsy duvh udrd dhoulf hsbr rcidyrf eiyh duvh trginrmrny
hr fif noy hrdiysyr sd yo yhr voutdr ihr esd yo putdur
the dpsnidh volonisl hidyoty
to hold to this communivsion
nsvk yo yhr brddrld
yhr duvvrddion esd vonyrnyrf
yhr glrry hrlf iyd voutdr
yhr golloeinh motninh

yhr mrn eotr s doty og s msnyir
ig you trgudr yhry vonvlufrf imiysiond yhr dyshr in ehivh
        for greater mortifications
likened to the note of a gong has survived however noble
yhr life of las cases hs been several times written
pudhrf on yhtrr 2o to5u 14wyu4e
llrlivi llrlfo
snoyhrt ysnk vondidyrf on s gull lion
vuy in yhr dolif tovk
        my bslusyiond og poryd hsbr trmsinrf ptryy vondysny

Out of all these various elements came the choruses that I performed with Adelle. The first of these was called "Overture: Chorus" because it was for me a genuine "opening." I wrote the poem in the 1970s and felt that I had discovered a powerful new form but I had no idea where or how it might be presented. Adelle and I performed "Overture: Chorus" at a friend's birthday party, where it was well received. (Someone there called it "the greatest poem I ever heard.") We didn't perform it again until 1985, when I did my first reading. Later that year, June 17, I did a reading at Larry Blake's Restaurant and Bar. I had been invited by the man who was really my discoverer, Iván Argüelles. Iván loved "Overture: Chorus" and encouraged me in all respects. I wrote a special new poem, "Sweeney Adrift"—another poem about a poem, in this case an ancient Irish one, *Buile Suibhne*—for our joint reading. As I wrote the poem, I kept phoning Iván to ask his advice: was it all right? He told me to keep it coming. I did. "Sweeney Adrift" begins,

welcome to the house of failure
see these are the structural bases of the house its beams and arteries
its artificial light its hands its vast appendices
who is
not here?
the range of things
delights us welcome welcome

see there is the door it opens for us
welcome

The joint reading was a great success, attended by a number of poets, including Philip Lamantia and Nancy Peters. Almost everyone attending had come to see Iván but both "Sweeney Adrift" and "Overture: Chorus" were very much appreciated. "Very original," Nancy Peters said to me. I was told by one attendee that the odd thing about my presentation was that I seemed like a "finished" poet, not a beginner, but no one had ever heard of me! "Performance" has been an important aspect of my life as a poet. It also seems to me an important development in the current history of poetry, and I have written about it in various essays and poems. Though I always had a strong sense of how the poem should sound, my awareness that "the page is not the / natural dividing point" was the beginning of a fully conscious perception. I recently read a very interesting dialogue between two well-known poets of different schools: I was surprised to see that the one thing they never discussed was performance. As for myself, I am grateful for my many opportunities to do readings and for the radio presentations I have done since 1986. Thank you, Berkeley, Oakland, San Francisco; thank you, KPFA.

Today's photos are Iván Argüelles reading at Larry Blake's in Berkeley on June 17, 1985 and the flyer for that reading.

SWEENEY ADRIFT
    for Iván Argüelles

welcome to the house of failure
see these are the structural bases of the house its beams and arteries
its artificial light its hands its vast appendices
who is
not here?
the range of things
delights us welcome welcome

see there is the door it opens for us
welcome

what sweeney what
have you done and
where have you done it?
sweeney clubbed the man
not once but twice; bashed his head in, hurt
him badly. Oh,
Sweeney they'll
not stand for that surely—   cf. *Buille Suibhne*
surely that's   trans. J.G. O'Keefe, 1913
no way to behave—   trans. Seamus Heaney, 1984
Sweeney
ended his tirade
his wild life then—
They all said, Enough, enough, Sweeney,
surely that's
no way
for a man to behave
Sweeney
kicked his eyes out hurt him broke his ribs twisted the tongue not
once but twice
bones broke, brittle for Sweeney, his trophy, taken, the life taken,
the balls
bashed

the life
ended
oh Sweeney
she bespoke him sorely oh
and Sweeney repented then
turned churchman spoke vows made retreats novenas bled holy
water ended his wild life
told tales made miracles believed end-
ed his wild life turned goodman churchman died of age and
soul
now surely turned—
to
heav'n.
sweeney.

SUN-

the slow turn of resolving
        moved (as ever) us (as ever) if
        (stay)

I go out again with
        money in my pockets

click!

how many times have I
asked you—spoken your
name—in this darkness—
I have nothing to offer—
in the air—endless
variations—*speech*!—

Bear
    turns—
open to the
    light—

She stopped for a moment and looked back. It is not easy to tell.

They saw each other only momentarily. It was not easy to tell.

Your book is…

> a big crazy delicious effort, fundamentally great, highly
> interesting, jocular, kinky, lovely, magnificently nice,
> opulent, pretty, quick, redolent, snazzy, tricky, undoubtedly
> very whimsical Xmas yummy. Zounds!

The night came, and a storm, and Sweeney's misery and mania

were so great that he cried out:

I who have neither another nor now
in the dim light (love)
          possibly
  frame (make) this (how) (love) quick

"I wrow rowe wrote chu
yesterday"—

Sweeney returns, and the lies about his son's death have caused

him to

All day, all night,
Sweeney clings
  to the branch, and opens
          (spreads his)
                    wings

He is now
          "adrift"—

(spoken to—

    uneasy in the night—
                  pressure—)

              Remember this, "friend"—
              hand extended—

is the problem presence?
    what does it matter if we love each other?
is the problem presence?
    what does it matter if we love each other?
is the problem presence?
    what does it matter if we love each other?
is the problem presence?
    what does it matter if we love each other?

bear
    the bear-son
opes
    his eyes

the "master of the mountain" is of special interest to us as he is the "master" of the bears. On the one hand he is a man, on the other, a real bear, only of unusually large size. All other bears are his fellow tribesmen…The slaughter of a bear represents the departure of the soul of the animal to its master and a subsequent return to earth is expected…It is not to the beasts themselves that offerings and prayers are made but to their "masters" or "owners"

"grandfather"… "old man"… "he"…Taking the skin off a slain bear they say, "Grandfather, owner of the earth, don't think ill of us. we did not do this to you. The Yakut did it. Your silver bones we shall put in a special house."

fish-dragon
blind and eyeless
naked as a
human finger
Sweeney

pueblo—bridge—creek—
cameras
clicking—old woman—looking—
eyes: thinking—

"We're going to have lunch with the guy who published *Nailed to the Coffin of Life*. His name is Loss Glazier."
"His name is Loss?"
"Yes."   "Lunch With Loss"
"We're going to have lunch with Loss?"
"Yes."
"I've been having Lunch with Loss for most of my life."

the bear has always been the weather prophet because he presages
by his emergence the
return of spring
to the
wintry
world

Juan, Juan el Oso, Juan del Oso, Ivanko the Bear's son—

Since matter itself is in a state of flux and is deprived of that form through which it takes shape and is made manifest, they took the dampness and humidity of caves, their darkness, and, as the poet says, their "murkiness," as an appropriate symbol for the properties of the cosmos the Persian mystagogues initiate their candidate by explaining to him the downward journey of souls and their subsequent return, and they call the place where this occurs a "cave"—

descending paralysis
bull
lord of *genesis*

sun—
　　　　shadow—

there is
blood on my face—

fuck it you know that fuckin cocksucker you know what that fucker said to me

Sweeney picked himself up off the hardbitterdesolatefrozen ground.
Again.

"Mother, would you *please* answer the door. I've been standing here for fifteen minutes."
"Couldn't be helped. I was on the shitter."　　—neighborhood
　　　　　　　　　　　　　　　　　　　　　　　　music

what does it mean to use the word *fuck*?

"Sleep a little, love,
　　　　　　　for thou needst nor fear the least"—

"I am Sweeney alas!
my wretched body is utterly dead—
A year have I been on the mountain
　　　　without music, without sleep—
Madman

am I—"

John Anson wrote a hundred rounds
As I have written only one.
O listen as his name resounds:
        John Anson.

My little round might be the sun.
The planets in their daily rounds   around the roundel
Must circle it in unison.

His trope might be the separate gowns
Of long-dead ladies now at one.
These separated, joining sounds:
        John—
                Ann's son.

how many times have I
asked you—spoken your
name—in this darkness—
I have nothing to offer—
in the air—endless
variations—speech—

It was night. The heat was still glutinous and no wind stirred. The
whirling "deedees" died away to the east as the glowing orange orb
of the sun drifted to the west in a purple miasma. (A narrative of
ideas not of *events*.)

And, Orpheus, will you bring your mother with you?—

field   piece   violence   cob   decoration   porcupine   brogan
finch   zeppelin   permeate   convent   artifact   behemoth   climax
ranger   pin   mens rea   brand   convent   jitter   own   as   bell

man   scatter   which   saddle   strange   blend   peace   orphan
spatch   poll   boing   infant   such   enter   hone   savor   claim
once   ping

Rhea—

—Why have you followed me   (Here the Hag speaketh
here?   with Sweeney
—*Yes*   and telleth him
—What have you come to tell me?   nothing.)
—*Yes.*

THE DEEP AND ABIDING MISERY OF THE MAD!
it was all sorrows   love's seeking
in a bloodless ending   still steeping
Sorrow, be neither stow(n)e nor still
it was blunt weeping
—The fly Augusta, the little imp
teases your nose and your forehead.
When one is a fly one is not an eagle
but one knows how to walk on the ceiling.
Pierre Febvre…Yes, Pierre Febvre. Why should I think of him, and
wonder what my spirit will make of him, feeling as I now do. His
face—
O obstinate mysteries
innocent animality!
You, simple house-fly
and you—foxes, crows, panthers,
creatures in whom the impulse to bite exuberates—
But I understand now how it is possible to muse upon the outline
of a nostril
or the curve of a lip for hour upon hour and never be satisfied.
Ha! Ha! Ha! Difference of sex makes for clear-sightedness, eh?
The street was dark; the Square was deserted;
the morning sun was still
and did not rise. "Sweeney—?"

Nevertheless I spent less time on the opening caresses in order to
get to the concluding ones with which we had just become
acquainted.
I lie upon the grass and see the sky. Her dress
billowed in the wind.
He sits for hours staring at the sea.
The way your breasts move as you move—the strangeness of it
It is the woman's part
to touch the
hand
to let you know   she *wishes*   to be touched—
August-
a thrives in the summer's carrion—
The relationship
                between the self-discovering mind and the world,
between the self-discovering mind and others, is one of *analogy*. I
can "find" myself not by looking inward but by looking outward
(invidia, envy, mania)
He stared upon the table on which a knife a fork and a spoon had
been carefully arranged
There are, uh, times I forget
I meant to
to forget
times   I do not want to
to
remember
"It's possible he has another reason for acting as he does. It's
possible he genuinely has something to hide."

Dawn light
mechanical and
human figures
catch the light

Think not, revolted Spirit, thy shape the same,
Or undiminisht brightness, to be known

As when thou stood'st in Heav'n upright and pure (thrives in the summer's carrion)
sunlight? here?   through a single
shaft
What are the names of the Seven Dwarfs?   —loneliness at the
Slothful, Envious, Lustful, Wrathful, Shameless…   shopping mall
contradictions   explanations
you who turn the wheel—

…an immense Being who alone remains eternal amidst the continual change and ceaseless transformation of all that constitutes him…

are you as good at sex as you are at literature?

For he whose mind is fixed upon true being has surely no time to look down upon the affairs of earth or to be filled with malice and envy, contending against men; his eye is ever directed towards things fixed and immutable, which he sees neither injuring nor injured by one another, but all in order moving according to reason; these he imitates, and to these he will, as far as he can, conform himself.

—you complain about "obscurity"
and assert that my poetry
is overly "intellectual."
You assume in saying this
that however complicated
"intellectual"
matters may be, in matters of
"emotion"
you stand with the poet
on common ground.
But is it not possible

that the poet has
felt something which you have not yet
felt
or have not yet recognized as
feeling
that it is an emotional
not an intellectual
"obscurity"
to which you object?

And now, I said, let me show in a figure how far our nature is enlightened or unenlightened. Imagine mankind living in a cave with a long entrance open to the light; in this they have been since childhood.

A "friend" is a relative. To "have right" expresses an obligation. About half the families have horse-drawn mowing machines. Those who have them mow their own meadows, working from earliest morning as long as light holds. They work with the aid of their sons and of boys from the families which have no machines. At each stage of the process a boy not a member of the family gives his labour and takes his place at meals during the day.

"I am patriotic and it may be a bad thing to say but I think that the school system they have now is bad and that the teaching of Irish is bad. In my day and before, a man might go to school when he could—maybe for only three months in the year. But he would know more then than they get now when they go to school all the time. The old people learned more then too. When a child finished school he would be expected to read a newspaper to the old people or to write a letter for them or to do sums. And he would do it well." ...a system which to his mind makes no provision for the mutuality between young and old...

and when one of them is liberated and compelled suddenly to stand up and turn his neck round and walk and look towards the light he will suffer sharp pains; the glare will distress him, and he will be unable to see the realities of what in his former state he had seen only as shadows

Things are "cast adrift," more or less like one another without any of them being able to claim the privileged status of "model" for all the rest—

Sweeney moved amongst the branches making a tremendous sound in the / head which listens—

> How is talk measured, love—   Beyond the obvious—
> "stained" words—
> restrained—
> heart's clue
> spoken

"Continual changes...are...every instant...occurring...to every... man"

epi-logos

...I would never have by myself undertaken the task of establishing such a collection and, grateful as I am to Bill Germano for his initiative, I confess that I still look back upon it with some misgivings. Such massive evidence of the failure to make the various individual readings coalesce is a somewhat melancholy spectacle. The fragmentary aspect of the whole is made more obvious still by the hypotactic manner that prevails in each of the essays taken in isolation, by the continued attempt, however ironized, to present a closed and linear argument. This apparent coherence *within* each essay is not matched by a corresponding coherence *between* them. Laid out diachronically in a roughly chronological sequence, they do not evolve in a manner that easily allows for dialectical progression or, ultimately, for historical totalization. Rather, it seems that they always start again from scratch and that their conclusions fail to add up to anything. If some secret principle of summation is at work here, I do not feel qualified to articulate it and, as far as the general question of romanticism is concerned, I must leave the task of its historical definition to others. I have myself taken refuge in more theoretical inquiries into the problems of figural language. Not that I believe that such a historical enterprise, in the case of romanticism, is doomed from the start: one is all too easily tempted to rationalize personal shortcoming as theoretical impossibility and, especially among younger scholars, there is ample evidence that the historical study of romanticism is being successfully pursued. But it certainly has become a far from easy task. One feels at times envious of those who can continue to do literary history as if nothing had happened in the sphere of theory, but one cannot help but feel somewhat suspicious of their optimism. *The Rhetoric of Romanticism* should at least help to document some of the difficulties it fails to resolve…. (Paul de Man, 1983)

Los Angeles, by its absence
dominates everything—
Sharp-eyed lynxes
watch us: Goyim?

How can one
begin

To think of you I

move

        "Hello, Tiny"

In the evening, in the rain—
      of birds
     a harvest-
         wealth-

NOTES

This poem is a fantasia based on a medieval Irish poem called *Buile Suibhne. Buile Suibhne* was translated first by J.G. O'Keefe in 1913 as *Sweeney the Mad* and then by Seamus Heaney in 1984 as *Sweeney Astray*. My poem is not a translation, but I do use the Irish poem as the basis for themes and variations of my own. Some sources: A. Irving Hallowell, *Bear Ceremonialism in the Northern Hemisphere;* Herbert Wendt, *Out of Noah's Ark;* Tony Moffeit's poem, "Those Who Speak Do Not Know Those Who Know Do Not Speak," *Oro Madre*, vol. 2, nos. 3-4; Rhys Carpenter, *Folktale, Fiction and Saga in the Homeric Epics; Funk & Wagnalls Standard Dictionary of Folklore, Mythology and Legend* (the article on the "Bear's Son"); Robert Lamberton's translation of Porphyry's essay, *On the Cave of the Nymphs;* Iván Argüelles' poem, "Descending Paralysis"; Kathleen Hoagland, *1000 Years of Irish Poetry;* Iván T. Sanderson, *The Continent We Live On;* Georges Norge, "Les Innocents" from *La Belle Saison* (I have translated only part of this poem); Jules Romains, *The Body's Rapture*, translated by John Rodker; some of my own very early poetry; John Milton, *Paradise Lost*, Book VI; Alexis de Tocqueville, *Democracy in America* (the Henry Reeve text as revised by Francis Bower); Plato, *The Republic*, Books VI and VII (I used both the Jowett and the Rouse translations); Conrad Arensberg, *The Irish Countryman;* James Harkness' introduction to his translation of Michel Foucault's *This is Not a Pipe;* Paul de Man's introduction to his *The Rhetoric of Romanticism*. The second passage in the epilogue was written while listening to Charlie Parker ("of birds / a harvest- / wealth"). John Anson is a friend of mine who published a sequence of a hundred roundels,

Sessions and Surroundings: A Century of Roundels. I responded to his sequence with my one. My proper name is "John," and my mother's name was a variant of "Ann," so I am in a sense "John, Ann's son."

DAY EIGHT

"The great poets have always mastered the rules then gone beyond them. We would not have a Walt Whitman, as we know him, had he not broken all rules of writing poetry. Whitman opened up the line and created a new kind of poetry, as big as America."

—Clarence Major, "Painting and Poetry"

...

We think of "prose" as the opposite of "poetry," as in the words "prosaic" and "poetic." I think it would be more accurate to think of prose as the opposite of verse. Prose is a *form*, as the sonnet or the villanelle is a form. Poetry, on the other hand, is a musical intensification of language in which words leap beyond themselves, affirming contexts beyond the immediate one in which they appear, beyond even what appears to be "meaning." As such, "poetry" may occur in either verse or prose; conversely, a particular sonnet or villanelle, though verse, might not be poetry, might not be a "poem," only verse. If James Joyce is not a poet in works like *Ulysses* and *Finnegans Wake*, I don't know what he is.

Yet he is writing "prose." How much "verse" does not qualify as "poetry"? Can we transform even autobiography into poetry?

***

Though I have included much in this eight-day presentation, much has necessarily been left out. I have not discussed my "writing between the lines," a technique I have been practicing for some time now. The first of these poems was called "Bukowski." I wrote this about it: I wrote this poem in response to a poem in Charles Bukowski's book, *Mockingbird, Wish Me Luck*. The words in the first, third, fifth, etc. lines are Bukowski's poem; the words in italics are by me. When I perform the poem, I speak the Bukowski portion in my "normal" voice; I speak the words by me in a whisper. I call this way of responding to a poem "writing between the lines."

Here is the poem:

the mockingbird had been following the cat
there was this cat
all summer
and I only saw him
mocking mocking mocking
once
teasing and cocksure;
when he gave a
the cat crawled under rockers on porches

reading
tail flashing
and burped
and said something angry to the mockingbird
at the audience
which I didn't understand.

yesterday the cat walked calmly up the driveway
and he read this poem
with the mockingbird alive in its mouth,
about a cat
wings fanned, beautiful wings fanned and flopping,
and a bird
feathers parted like a woman's legs,
and he was both
and the bird was no longer mocking,
the cat and
it was asking, it was praying
the bird
but the cat
and he was devouring
striding down through centuries
himself
would not listen.
through the poem.

I saw it crawl under a yellow car
And I listened
with the bird
letting him die
to bargain it to another place.

summer was over.
Bukowski.

Here is a later poem juxtaposing two passages I myself wrote:

DUET WITH MYSELF

The function of memory
My name is Jack
is to soften the blow of death
I was born
to create the illusion of a self
far away
though it is also memory
on the east coast
that creates
of america
the fear of death
in a city near the roaring sea

This is the function
I live
of memory:
now
to soften
in the far, far west
the blow of death
near
to create
the roaring
the illusion
of another
of self
sea

Such poems, I believe, like much of my work, are ways of bringing *world*, rather than simply the lyrical ego, into the poem. They insist on the "multiple" aspect of even the supposedly "personal" lyric form. They are a reflection of one of the twentieth century's deepest notions: the perception that some parts of the mind don't know what other parts of the mind are doing though all may be equally active—the perception that mind itself is complex, multiple, kaleidoscopic, even contradictory. Isn't that the kind of world that emerges from Shakespeare's plays? We usually speak of multiplicity as a social phenomenon—the diverse ethnic groups in the United States, for example. But it seems to me that we see what we are, that it is the multiple aspect of our minds that allows us to see multiplicity in the world. I have no problem with the notion of "the individual" as a political fact: the rights of the individual are everywhere to be respected. But I do have a problem with that notion as a fact of mind. The word "individual" is from the Latin *in-dividuus*, not divisible, not divided. It seems to me that, on the contrary, mind is deeply divided, that being divided is its constant condition. If that's so, I can hardly be categorized as an "individual." I must be something else. My word for that something else is "multiplicity"—though I would not deny the fact that every human being is unique. How can poetry, even lyrical poetry, express that situation? One answer to that question is to keep your work constantly *collaborative*, even when, as in the case of the Bukowski poem, the person you're collaborating with is completely unaware of your presence. "World"—and "collaboration"—may be present in the form of history, including the history of particular words—what T.S. Eliot called "the historical sense." It may be present in the form of the translation of a poet who wrote in another language.

My friend Iván Argüelles—with whom I have actively collaborated in two books—is very much aware that I may "respond" at any moment to the work he sends me daily. I found this to be one of his most moving poems, and I answered it immediately:

IVÁN ARGÜELLES ON HIS DECEASED SON MAX, WHO SUFFERED SINCE THE AGE OF NINE WITH ENCYPHALITIS AND WHO WAS CARED FOR LOVINGLY, AT HOME, BY HIS PARENTS, IVÁN AND MARILLA

EMPTY DAYS : *MAX* IN ABSENTIA

the surgeon and coroner play solitaire with left hands
words are only unuttered breaths the sentiment
that *all* is only part of the half we should realize
before the hour is up conjecture of a mythic sunset
mire and morass of thought wrapped and put
into a storage box and futility of endeavor silence
best expressed with vowels borrowed from a liturgy
religious exercises in the tumulus and a brief
association with light whatever else matters is
small comfort to the survivors whose senses remain
the property of a flawed deity a smoking height
a distance of compounded grief and hills evaporating
in the window's ominous reflections come nightfall
to think that his breath straddled two *centuries !*
memories when he was OK nine years old pedaling
his bike to Brooklyn Heights and back and silly

games and tiny sounds of syllables and allocations
of sudden happiness and ropes of rhyme and air
such it was when archaic rock and sediment
turned to blank quarters of an inchoate dream
unimaginable hues resonances *disorder* of space
this day these days this era of disease and manipulation
headlines full of catastrophic ciphers and delusions
freight trains stuck in glacial seasons without reprieve
a hundred thousand seconds counted backwards
between a pair of unnamed avenues and lock-downs
what's to live for what's the gain in salvation ?
there are no numbers greater or less than *Three* !
knowledge is a discarded brick and information a lie
the almighty Zeus of epic a lingering smoke in doubt
what's come and gone and been translated is a hoax
sheets out to dry the past is in the missing sky
to grieve and mourn to fix the mind in old re-runs
to rearrange the furniture and knit new crosswords
asleep in a distance which is already here
look to the grass that hasn't grown for years
search the concrete in front for a solitary silhouette
memory is a repercussion between deaf ears like
the glint of sea in the mortician's eye an echo of salt
unplayed games doors without knobs speechless leaves
and *Max* a shadow on the wall when no one's looking

12-02-20

I answered:

tears
my dear friend
tears
here in my crowded den
surrounded by books
& memories

& memories of books
tears because I saw Max live
saw his joy to see his father
to know he was loved
and had someone to love
beyond that, who knows
but that should be enough
for any of us
any of us who go through years
on this loving, benighted planet
enough to know
we loved
and were loved
though we were not perfect

though we vanished like smoke or wind

12/03/20

I've also written poems in *scriptio continua*—an ancient practice to preserve space on the page that I felt might have expressive possibilities—but I will get to that later.

As I mentioned earlier, "Performance" is large issue of my work. There is a famous passage in Book Six of Augustine's *Confessions*. Augustine is watching St. Ambrose in the act of reading, and he notices something which is, to him, quite remarkable. "When [Ambrose] was reading," writes St. Augustine, "his eye glided over the pages, and his heart searched out the sense, but his voice and tongue were at rest." Augustine sensed at that moment that a momentous change had come upon the world.

In his experience, it was often the case that if a book was "read," it was read aloud to a group of people—listeners. This was not true of Ambrose. In addition, Ambrose was reading without moving his lips and without making a sound. Unlike the Homeric "singer," he was not in the least "performing": he was moving only his eyes. Augustine suddenly understood that the "new" consciousness was Christian, inward, and silent before the page. Augustine's "new" consciousness is also *our* consciousness. We are taught to read like Ambrose—without moving our lips and without making a sound. Indeed, in a writing culture, verse, with its considerable interest in sound, is regarded as a kind of atavism—a mode of far less importance than prose. In our culture, "meaning" trumps "music." My work is in a way a challenge to all of that. I regarded Adelle and me as the *un* Saint Ambrose: we were reading a text but we were directing it *outward*, towards an audience. "Homophonic" work like Louis Zukofsky's *Catullus* was also an insistence on sound—a development that came hand in hand with the arising of what we call "the media."

Since Adelle's death in 2016, the changes in my life have been many, though many things have remained the same. The presence in my life of Sangye Land continues to be a great joy. If there were a ninth day, she would be celebrated there—though there is a section devoted to her in my book, *When Sleep Comes: Shillelagh Songs* and she is a frequent performer on my radio show.

I want to end these presentations with two poems which come as close as I can come to summarizing my current situation. The word "expoesis"—a kind of equivalent to "ekphrastic"—is my coinage. My poem is not about a visual work of art: it's about a poem.

WHITMAN'S "OUT OF THE CRADLE ENDLESSLY ROCKING" (EXPOESIS)

I don't think there is another *poem*
More unique
And, simultaneously,
More representative of
What we may call the American spirit
Than this amazing
Presentation of the making of a poet
Of the transformation of anyone
From childhood to a condition of knowledge
How do we enter the world in a deep way
It is an aria, a performance
Something Whitman saw in the opera houses,
It is a multi-voiced, multi-selved poem in which
All sorts of styles and "voices" are brought together
(Including the hissing voice of the old crone, the sea, and the voice
of the bird, "my dusky demon and brother," "the lone singer
wonderful")
It is a poem about family (the he-bird, the she-bird)
It is a poem about the stunning fact of Death the Opener
And the great representation of the sea (Melville)
(The sea is the openness of consciousness)
It is a nature poem
In which the "outsetting bard" merges with what he sees
It includes Quakers ("Ninth-month midnight")
And Native Americans ("Paumanok")

It is Whitman giving himself over to the sheer possibilities of
music
As world becomes word ("translating")
It is an act of marvelous empathy and compassion in the literal
sense, "feeling with"
It is a poem about the body and its transformation
Even as Whitman speaks of the soul
It is a poem in which the lorn bird and the transforming boy
Move us to what Wallace Stevens called
A new representation of reality.
This, camerados, is the great mythic moment of American letters
And it takes place not at a desk but outside,
Not as writing but as brilliant spontaneous unexpected utterance.
It ushers in (under the magical multivalent moon, in the presence
of the vast, talkative sea)
Nothing less than the world as song.

...

AT EIGHTY

at eighty I have left
a long paper trail
despite a late start
how many books
17 of poetry alone
but there are others
and they are sometimes
rather long
it's a complex life I've led
a life of dreams
and commentary
Freud, Jung, Heidegger
my guides
to say nothing of Cole Porter,

Lorenz Hart, Noël Coward, Laurel & Hardy,
Johnny Mercer, Bernard Shaw, Delmore Schwartz, Michel Butor
(*Mobile*),
George M. Cohan, Shakespeare, Marlowe, Thomas Wolfe, *The
Indians' Book*,
Hannah Arendt, Gertrude Stein, "Germs' Choice," Jean Toomer,
Fred Astaire,
Dante, Virgil, Milton, Hammett, Waugh, Groucho Marx, Spicer,
Lao Tsu, Brassens, Piazzolla, Olson, Duncan, Jess, dear Larry
Eigner, Langston Hughes, Hitchcock, Abel Gance, Pound, Eliot,
Bashō, Baudelaire, Rimbaud, Sandburg, Williams, The Beatles,
Les Paul, Muddy Waters, Sartre, de Beauvoir, Cocteau, McClure,
Dylan Thomas, Whitman, Grahn, Beckett, Baldwin, Kerouac,
Shelley, Thomas Gray, Lorca, Melville, Poe, Elinor Wylie, Ted
Joans, Frost, Brecht, Yeats, Paul de Man, Charles Ives, Lou
Harrison, Rilke, Gershwin, Purcell, Dickinson, Emerson, a man on
the street whose name I don't remember, so many others.
I don't believe
in "coming of age" as in
"a coming of age story"
I don't believe in linear development
but rather in a vast, circling, endless
consciousness in which new things
are constantly added but which
is more chaotic than anything else and goes
as my friend James Broughton said,
"beautifully nowhere."
We are a vastness
that pretends to be finite.
80 Flowers is a book
by Louis Zukofsky
who did not live to be eighty.
His book, and the marvelous title,
outlived him.
I will take the title
on August 9, 2020
and feel the flowering of my age.

Thank you, wonderful Zukofsky
whom an ignorant, famous poet
once insisted was "terrible, just terrible."
Imagination
flowers at eighty
in perhaps a way that it did not
when I was young.
These years, these memories,
these fictions
fly from me as I stay
at the center of an ocean
in which I tread water
until the perhaps benevolent
darkness
calls to me and says,
"Come"—not home, just
"Come."

I note, incidentally, that Zukofsky's word "flowers" is both a noun and a verb. Today's photo is a recent attempt at a kind of self portrait, complete with microphone. Pencil, ink, Crayola.

"I write, write, write as the Wandering Jew walks, walks, walks."
—Helena Blavatsky

POST SCRIPT

This poem is part of a recent sequence called "Orphic Sonnets." It is perhaps a fitting conclusion to this section of my "backward glance o'er travel'd roads."

ORPHIC SONNET #23
("How many times, in dreams, Eurydice...")

How many times, in dreams, Eurydice...
The women came for me...brandishing knives...
Struggling to get near me, to be the first to kill.
I could not speak

One grabbed for my throat, others stabbed,
Everywhere, my arms, my stomach, my chest,
My heart, my back! I could not speak.
Screaming, in the violent fit they were,

As they went about their ghastly business of murder.
Finally, they chopped my head off and tossed it in the river
Which ran red with my blood.
                    And then suddenly

My tongue began to sing, but it was not human words
Words of the dead, which no human understands,
The birds sang with me, as my head flowed on and on

Sdnatsredun namuh on hcihw daed eht fo sdrow...
Thebirdssangwithme,asmyheadflowedonandon...
eotffd og yhr frsf, ehivh no humsn unfrtdysnfd...
- -

COMMENTARIES: RANDOM THOUGHTS ON THE ART OF POETRY AND ON A FEW OTHER THINGS, TOO

Old man, old man,
what can you say
when the night comes down upon you

*

FORMAL POEM BEGINNING WITH LINES BY STEVENS

"If men at forty will be painting lakes
The ephemeral blues must merge for them in one,
The basic slate, the universal hue.
There is a substance in us that prevails."

If men at eighty will be writing poems
They will tell stories of their long, long lives
They will attempt a summary of sorts.
There is a substance in us that prevails.

Or is there? Is it longing that we feel,
This certainty? I was a man of forty
But that was forty years ago, and now
I am a traveller in the realm of thought

Or is it time? I was a child once long,
Long ago. But I remember still

An elevation of my childish mind,
A sudden ecstasy of comprehension

In which time stopped, though time was hurrying.
I am a man of eighty writing poems
That seem to be an exercise in love
Yet may be nothing but a way for me

To trick my soul. I am a traveller
Who moves from world to world and back again
And flies on words but scarcely moves at all.
I am the moving shadow on the wall.

...

THE DICTIONARY

He spent his life
In the compilation of a dictionary
This dictionary was an endlessly incomplete
Record of everything he had said
And everything that had been said to him
And every thought he had had
And everything he had read and seen
It was all words nothing but vowels and consonants
Words seen words spoken words he had dreamed
On endless nights when his thoughts turned
Restlessly half forgotten
Words
It was a book and not
A book his word for it was poetry
But really it was nothing but a dictionary
The words that had clung to him as he lived
Among flowers and trees and cities and people
And air and rain and grief and joy and

The sudden understanding
That all words led out of themselves

.

Into nothing *into the way reality*

Was present to the endless fountain of his mind.

...

GATE, GATE, PARAGATE, PARASAMGATE, BODHI SVAHAA!

Going, going, going on beyond
Always going on beyond,
Always becoming Buddha
Going, going,
Going on beyond,
Beyond this beyond
The
Always going on
Always becoming
Buddha
In the dark of our lives
This song
Awakens life
Awakens me to longing
A longing song that rises
In the heart of the morning in the sudden flush of love for
Sangye
As I see the Buddha
Not as a person but as a possibility
As the never ending
Always beginning

Always going on
Beyond
Arising in my heart   *arising*
In the deep ground
Of being

PAUL DE MAN

I have been reading Evelyn Barish's attack biography of that
scoundrel, Paul de Man, with whom I studied in the 1960s.
Fascinating. What scrapes he got himself into. He embezzled funds
from a publishing house he was involved in, lied his way into
Harvard, was technically a bigamist, sheltered Jews, wrote anti
Semitic articles for a newspaper published by his uncle Henri de
Man, who was a Belgian collaborationist. His past was constantly
almost catching up with him. Yet the sheer brilliance of his mind
impressed everyone who ever came across him—me included. It
was a wonderful thing to watch him unfold a poem, a piece of
writing. He was, in the deepest sense, a storyteller, a creator of
fables. Sometimes the subject of the fables was a poem; sometimes
it was his own immensely problematical life. The biographer
seems to know nothing of his rejection of his life's work in *The
Rhetoric of Romanticism*—though she certainly accounts for the
anxiety I noticed: a constant assertion that sometimes you publish
something before you should—and you feel shame. She
understands the almost comic way his past kept nipping at his
heels, but she doesn't seem to understand the sense of shame. A

life lived as an always threatened fiction. What stories he told. How he could épater le bourgeois! He knew his consciousness was shot through with fiction, with fantasy, yet he understood that that was the nature of consciousness—of all consciousness. His brilliant, illuminating stories kept him one jump ahead of insidious reality—a reality which he himself had largely created! He was a bounder, a liar, a man not to be trusted, yet in a deep sense he was a lamp. He evidently spent hours gazing at himself in mirrors. His surname means simply "The Man." What an enigma "the man" is—man is. Life—founded on nothing but lies, fictions. Yet fascinating, beautiful—not to be held down by anything. Insight is piled upon insight in his thought, he lives his life for insight, yet he believes that every insight carries with it a fundamental blindness which the thinker can never penetrate. One longs for truth, but every truth carries with it its own particular falseness. Truth and untruth are a pair that can never be separated. To be human is to tell stories. But stories are fictions. And fictions are lies.

The emotion I feel when I think about him is one of joy.

"If I had it to do over again," he said to his son, "I would have been rich."

Bounder/untrustworthy/opener of doors.

*

THE DDD MONSTER

The DDD Monster was worried.

He wanted very much to be a part of the family he was living with but he wasn't sure exactly where he fit in. Most families have mothers, fathers, children, relatives, dogs, cats, goldfish—but monsters? How did monsters fit into a family? He tried to calm himself by extending his forefinger and poking it gently into the sofa three times while saying "DDD," which is how he got his name. Nobody, including the monster, knew *why* he said "DDD" and poked things. He just said it and poked. Usually he liked to do this very much. It made him feel *very* good. So he tried again: "DDD." But it didn't help. He was still worried.

The Astronaut often assured the Monster that he was cared for, and the Monster always believed the Astronaut. But the Monster wanted more than assurance. He wanted to be a real member of the family, just as the Astronaut was. The Astronaut's father, Jack, would call the Astronaut "big boy" and "my son." Who was there to call the DDD Monster such names? Maybe monsters didn't have families.

"Shut up, D," said the Astronaut, walking into the room. That was the Astronaut's way of greeting the Monster. The Monster liked it because it meant the Astronaut had noticed him. Usually the greeting made the Monster say something. But today he was more than usually sad. "Thank you, Sean," he said—he always thanked the Astronaut when the Astronaut told him to shut up—but he said nothing more.

"What's the matter, Monst?" asked Sean, who noticed the Monster's sadness.

"Wah," said the Monster. "I'm not a member of the familyyyyyyy. Wah."

Sean poked the Monster to cheer him up. "DDD," he said. Usually this made the monster feel *very* good. But today it didn't seem to work.

"I tell you what, Monst," said Sean. "Let's go ask Jack whether you're a member of the family. He'll be sure to know."

So the Astronaut and the Monster went in search of Jack, the Astronaut's father.

from my story, "The Monst," available in my book, The Tiger and Other Tales

*

IRISH AMERICAN

What does it mean to be Irish? Or, more specifically, what does it mean to be Irish American?

To get from my house to Cornell University where I was a freshman in 1958, you drove up the hypotenuse of a right triangle. My father, who had been born in New York State farm country in 1895 and who grew up with the automobile, drove up the two sides of the triangle, thinking they were the hypotenuse. He never quite trusted that machine to get him where he wanted to go, and before any trip of consequence he would fortify himself with "a few drops of the craythur."

As we neared Cornell, there were several small towns which regularly made money at this time of year by giving tickets to students blazing through them on their way back to school. My father never blazed anywhere, but he did accidentally turn left through a red light as we slowly made our way to our goal. Suddenly a motorcycle policeman was upon us. The policeman said—and I don't exaggerate his brogue—"HO WHERE YA GOIN'?" My father pulled over to the side of the road and said very politely, "Gee, officer, did I go through that red light? I'm sorry. I won't do it again. Say," he said, "are you Irish?" The policeman flushed and said, rather testily, "Well, I'm Irish, what of it?" "Well," said my father, "we're Irish too. Meet the boy. We're taking him up to his freshman year at Cornell University."

My mother, who was Italian, said not a word.

By the time the conversation between my father and the policeman was over there was no longer any question of a ticket. The policeman was inviting us to his home for coffee and to "meet the wife." My father politely declined and said he would "drop by on the way back."

I have no idea whether my father even knew the name of the town whose laws he was violating, and I certainly do not. But when he heard that accent, he knew exactly how to behave. He acknowledged the policeman's authority: "Gee, officer, did I go through that red light? I'm sorry. I won't do it again." But he then invoked a *higher* authority: "Are you Irish?"

There was a joke my father liked to tell, and perhaps its moral figured in that Irish cop's reaction to us. The Irish maid is about to leave for the day when the master says to her, "Mary, this is terrible. Look at the dust on this table. I can write my name in the dust." "Oh, sir," she says, misunderstanding, "ain't education grand!" Perhaps the thought of "education," and particularly education for the Irish, was "grand" for that Irish cop too. "Meet the boy," said my father proudly, "we're taking him up to his freshman year at Cornell University."

What does it mean to be Irish? What does it mean to be Irish American?

...

GABRIEL ROSENSTOCK AFTER READING MY
AUTOBIOGRAPHY:

Thanks, Jack,

A great read.

I can't quite figure out what you mean when you say your father
was Irish.

That would mean nothing over here without being more specific!

When did his people come over from Ireland? What townland, or
at the very least, what county did they hail from?

Sorry for being nosey but everyone here knows, for instance, that
Biden's people come from Ballina in Co. Mayo. Specific! It would
mean nothing, I'm afraid, to say 'Biden is Irish.'
Take care,

Gabriel

JACK:

That's interesting.

The specificities you mention probably arise out of the fact that
where you live, EVERYONE is Irish so other distinctions have to
be made.

Where I live, that isn't the case. Certainly, no such distinctions were made by the employers who sported NO IRISH NEED APPLY signs.

My father never spoke of the specifics of his heritage. It was always simply being Irish. If he saw a sign saying "Sullivan's Used Car Lot," for example, he'd exclaim, jokingly, "That's a damn fine used car lot, that Sullivan's! Go there!"

This was also true of my mother's side of the family. It was always "we're Italian"—not (what I found out many years after my mother's death) "we're Calabrese."

For Americans, it's a lot more important that Biden is Irish (and Catholic!) than that his people came from Ballina in Co. Mayo. Americans have probably never heard of Ballina in Co. Mayo but they have definitely heard of the Irish.

Jack

GABRIEL:

Thanks, Jack. We're all like little fiefdoms over here. Or smaller still. My wife said yesterday that it was raining.

She was looking out the front window. I said, it wasn't. I was looking out the back window and it wasn't raining there at all.

It's like this country has a few million psychic microclimates within a small space!

Your father's people more than likely came from the Decies in South East Ireland, a stronghold of the Foleys.
Take care,

Gabriel

JACK:

Bigod I never knew!

Thanks, Gabriel.

*

CATECHISM: ARGÜELLES TO FOLEY:
[from *Saint James: An Homage to James Joyce*]

What are imaginary girlfriends? That's what I say.
Are they the ones that stick like glue to the inside of your pants?
Yes. Hence Pantsograph. Requiring a "press."
Can you name any? Amy, Henrietta, whatever. They're imaginary, you can name them anything you like.
Have you ever had one? I have "had" all of them.
If so, what did you do with her? (Dreamily) Yes...

Did she react to your bristles? Only when I asked her to. I also reacted to hers.

Did she have any kind of a past? She had every kind of a past.

Was she always there when you needed her? She was always here when I needed her.

Did you ever "need" her? I do nothing but "need" her.

Were you on your knees for her? Naturally. How else can you clean the floor?

Did she knead you, but hard? Oh, hardly!

Did Mom and Dad faint when they met her?
They didn't but I did.

Was she worth trashing after a while? Sure.

Did she come back to haunt you in dreams? She never leaves my dreams.

Would you ever write a poem about her? Always do.

What kind of poem would "that" be? "That" poem.

Would you call it "Release me and let me love again?"
"and let me lust agayn"

Would you rather go to a monastery and study Thomism? I'd rather go to a monastery and study Madonna.

Do you still feel it was worth it?

I mean this imaginary life you call poetry?
Imaginary? Life?

After catechism, confession and release. Transformation. O
Whoolly Fatermutt, ringding my renaissance, it's been yares since
the last and maybe niver a gain, maybe only WARDS in thir
foibleness is all that ere exploded in this vacumm of mine
headpiece. Crusts for the cranium. Bliss me.

*

FOLEY TO ARGÜELLES
[from *Saint James: An Homage to James Joyce*]

To the Esteemed Le Terrible:

It's the Baddy Lairs
and the Bold old leery lusters
upchucking varses in drag
in the hinter regions
of the inter Knot
what sextrammeters!
what nudes of nuggets
what passover flyploys
what oyster messengers
(did I see a WING there
duck under
give it a gander
Bland blind St. Goosey is what a site!)
We goes on babblin and brooklyn
will we never seas the day
or the seasoning
oh ho there she goes with her drawers adroop
her panties a pied
(and me haven't peed for an hour
what air ya holdin it in for

is it the Second Cummings you're waiting for?)
Have we flayed the peacock yet?
I could use a feather, a quill (I will)
My Smile is my Simile
and I lost my—head—for Semele
beep beep are you waiting still
In the dank tarn I rant (my dank tarn rant)
My hair will cost me, Vera—aver!
See it fall
Is that all
Bal
d bald
like a sweet young thing before puberty
(my tarn rant is tart!)
A true tail: I farted the other day
and the wife said:
"What did you say dear?"
It must have been a remark
of unusual
intelligence
for Sunday
beep
and is there lightning out?
or is it lightening?
quick quick
you'll never get well if you swell
tumescence is turbulence sure
(that's my tokology)
The stones are bright
in the dimming light
and I died of fright.
Out with it!
Light! Light!
Out with it! Out with the
Liiiiiiiiiiiigggggggggghhhhhhhhhttttttttttttttttttttttttttttttttttttttttttttttttttttttttt
tttt

...

[I am naught but a poor relative of James Joyce: the great Irish liberator of the English landwish!--J. Foley]

*

PROSE FOR TWO VOICES
—Though I sleep as much as anyone else,

I am an advocate of being awake.

It had, he thought, a totemic resonance, that image of the woman suf-
   It had, he thought, a totemic resonance, that image
fering. (This happened later, before I could.) In the dark I thought of
   of the woman suffering. (This happened later, before I could.)
her. How can you say that she asked. How can you say that. Undulate,
   In the dark I thought of her. How can you say that she asked.
fish. I spoke to her for about fifteen minutes. This is the guarded situ-
   How can you say that. Undulate, fish. I spoke to her for about
ation. I am in my thoughts. This is a recollection of last night when we
   fifteen minutes. This is the guarded situation. I am in my
all saw a film. I wanted. Children sound and resound. The image of a
   thoughts. This is a recollection of last night when we all saw
house, filled with happy children. What more than that. We'll all be in
   a film. I wanted. Children sound and resound. The image of a
that house he promised. We'll all be happy. Night darkens. Stains. I am
   house, filled with happy children. What more than that. We'll all
in the dream of the happy woman. Terrific! she said. As she crossed her
   be in that house he promised. We'll all be happy. Night darkens.

legs I thought: *The Renaissance.* Her lipstick turned her mouth into a

> *Stains. I am in the dream of the happy woman. Terrific! she
> said.*

scar. I adored him I adored him. Come. Now. I want to play ball. I

> *As she crossed her legs I thought:* The Renaissance. *Her
> lipstick*

want you to tell me how I can do it. I don't know. Whenever he opens his

> *turned her mouth into a scar. I adored him I adored him.
> Come. Now.*

mouth something happens. She was alone so she took off her dress. Now I

> *I want to play ball. I want you to tell me how I can do it. I don't*

am closing the door. I am opening the transit. Folie de doute. What a

> *know. Whenever he opens his mouth something happens. She
> was alone*

word! I saw you, don't deny it. She had (or so I thought) a totemic reso-

> *so she took off her dress. Now I am closing the door. I am
> opening*

nance, that image of the tall woman suffering.

> *the transit. Folie de doute. What a word! I saw you, don't deny
> it.*
> *She had (or so I thought) a totemic resonance, that image
> of the tall woman*
>
> > *suffering.*

*

ARTAUD: A PERFORMANCE PIECE

He walks in the spectacle
He was so handsome, très beau, vous savez

that is everything around him
And then ...et puis après...maigre...misère
Madly insisting on his
sanity and insanity
SCREAMING and insistent
that he is right
while knowing that he is in excess
and comic and *wrong*—
ironic, sincere,
and vastly accusatory
At once frail and full of authority
"Le *mômo*" qui *joue* le *mômo* pour ses amis artistiques de Paris
DON'T CURE ANYONE OF ANYTHING
CURING PEOPLE IS DEATH
DOCTORS ARE KILLERS
SCIENCE IS BLACK MAGIC
SCIENTISTS ARE BLACK MAGICIANS
WHOSE TOOLS ARE MADNESS AND ELECTRIC SHOCK
AND **PAIN!**
J'ai appris hier
(il faut croire que je retarde, ou peut-être n'est-ce qu'un faux bruit,
l'un de ces sales ragots comme il s'en colporte entre évier et
latrines à l'heure de la mise aux baquets des repas une fois de plus
ingurgités),
j'ai appris hier
l'une des pratiques officielles les plus sensationnelles des écoles
publiques américaines
et qui font sans doute que ce pays se croit à la tête du progrès.
Il paraît que parmi les examens ou épreuves que l'on fait subir à un
enfant qui entre pour la première fois dans une école publique,
aurait lieu l'épreuve dite de la liqueur séminale ou du
SPERME....
mo to ho he ah
mem zi ag oh toog
mama
mama
mômo mômo mômo

Commentaries: Random thoughts on the art of poetry
and on a few other things, too
103

et moi...toothless...addicted...mem zi ag oh toog
zi   zi

*

CONVERSATION DEALING WITH #POETMENOTLEAVE

JAKE BERRY: And so it began. In the middle of your life. You began appearing. The ironies are compiled. "Certain that nothing would come of it." "welcome to the house of failure" - both are openings to works that not only drew you out of depression, but also out of yourself, which is always where depression lurks and into the world you have inhabited ever since and received endless accolades and numerous awards for it - not to mention a body of work that is unlike and unmatched by anyone else. It took me a moment to recognize the fellow in the photo. Then I knew it was Iván, our prophet and guiding angel. A man whose voice roars still and who still enthusiastically communicates the poetry he finds important. And so it began. In the middle.

JACK TO JAKE: In medias res.

JAKE BERRY: You've made an exceptional series of it. I was surprised to read and learn much that I didn't know about you, and not surprised that I learned much about other things. I must say that in recent years I am returning to the ancient practice of reading most things aloud, or at least moving my lips and making some small sound. Increasingly, I want to hear what I read. Another thing I learned from you, long ago.

RAY MILLER TO JAKE BERRY: I always hear it in my mind's ear. I thought everyone did!

JACK TO RAY: The "voice" you "hear" in your mind's "ear" is a kind of echo of your impulse to speak the words aloud—to turn the letters on the page into words. It is a way of dealing with what is essentially a mode of repression: *don't speak the words aloud, read them with your eyes only.* It is generally assumed that writing can find some sort of equivalent for any speech act. But when my partner and I speak different words simultaneously there is no way for writing to represent the physical impact of that event, though of course the CD can do it easily. Once a second voice is brought into the presentation of poetry, poetry moves beyond writing. When poets tell you that poetry is rooted in speech—as in Auden's "poetry is memorable speech"—they do not mean speech by two or more people. They mean speech by one person—so that what they are saying is no different from saying that poetry is rooted in something that can be represented by writing very well; here, poetry and writing are more or less equivalent. But a second voice changes everything.

As for your suggestion that Jake, having written "Gossip," a wonderful poem of the interplay of voices, should try his hand at writing a play: I wouldn't put boundaries on anything Jake might wish to do, but I frequently make a distinction between a poem of "voices"—as in T.S. Eliot's magnificent poem, "The Waste Land" —and a play that has "characters"—as in Eliot's often rather dreadful dramatic pieces. The disembodied voices of a poem are not equivalent to characters in a drama—as Eliot found out when he tried to be a playwright. Eliot once groused that Noël Coward had never spent five minutes in the study of ethics. Coward replied that he didn't think that would have done him much good but that Eliot might have spent five minutes in the study of theater.

*

PEOPLE WHO TELL YOU THAT POETRY

is essentially speech
do not mean that
poetry is essentially speech
they mean that
poetry is essentially speech
by one person
that the poem is the utterance
of the "individual"—
the undivided self
they do not see speech
as multiple
do not follow
the many-voiced examples
of Whitman's
"Out of the Cradle Endlessly Rocking"

Eliot's
"The Waste Land"
Pound's
"Cantos"
do not see speech
as something that may be
opposed
to writing
as something
that writing cannot quite
capture
as something
in some senses freer
than writing: "winged" ...
so that speech for them
leads back to text
leads back to page
and not to tongue talk
not to action
not to what I am doing
at this very moment
though you cannot hear it
though your ears strain
and your voice catches
and you believe
that I am
writing

*

BOB DYLAN, COLE PORTER, AND RHYME

"Hey, Bob Dylan won the Nobel Prize for Literature."
    —A friend

A friend asked me for my opinion of Bob Dylan's effect on American poetry. It was a good question since so many of my poet friends write poetry but when they become emotionally engaged, generally talk about rock n roll. This was my answer:

The Dylan that meant most to me was the Dylan of the 1960s.

I think of him more as a songwriter—a very, very good songwriter—than as a poet, though of course song lyrics are a mode of poetry. (Think of Robert Burns.) Bob Dylan certainly has a gift for resonant, memorable phrases. And the fact that his immense verbal energy was able to touch so many people—was so *popular*—was definitely invigorating and cheering. I think it is important that the songs he wrote during the 60s had revolution as their central theme. I don't think that's true of his work anymore— that theme has dropped out—but it was definitely a factor in his popularity at that time of highly self-conscious, "revolutionary" "change." He seemed, along with a few others, to be the very voice of the 1960s. He obviously drew energy from Beat writing, but I'm not sure that his work had any effect on poetry as such—though certainly many American poets envied his capacity to interest millions in his work. If rock stars gained a kind of respectability by being called "poets," many people who were called poets longed for both the vast audiences and the immediacy of response that rock stars were able to achieve. Dylan seemed, then, an embodiment of freedom and hope. And he was *young*, as everybody was young in the 1960s. He was one of the people to whom Diane di Prima dedicated her book, *Revolutionary Letters*.

Dylan's impact on poetry probably had less to do with the quality or techniques of his work than it did with the fact that his work was *performed*. He was certainly a factor in the rise of "spoken word" or "performance poetry." The wonderful Alabama poet Jake Berry—whose work is highly experimental and contains many "performative" elements—sees Dylan as one of the people whose inspiration he most cherishes. Indeed, Berry is a songwriter/performer as well as a poet and sees no disconnect between songwriting and writing poetry. Berry's songs, like Dylan's, are rooted in folk music and the blues—though he has listened carefully to people like Miles Davis and has experimented with alternative tunings and various other things in his music. Neo Formalist poets—at the opposite pole from Berry—also often cite Dylan in their attempts to defend rhyme in poetry, though their actual work does not resemble Dylan's and, as far as I know, they don't write songs.

Here are a few thoughts, written a few years ago, about Dylan's effect on rhyme in songwriting:

Something happened to rhyming in popular songs in the late 1950s and 1960s. The famous Cornell professor M.H. Abrams used to give a regular lecture on how lyricists like Cole Porter, Ira

Gershwin, Irving Berlin, Lorenz Hart, etc. have their roots in "light" verse, which itself goes back to the 17th century. Sir John Suckling, for example:

Out upon it, I have lov'd
Three whole days together;
And am like to love three more,
If it prove fair weather.

Time shall moult away his wings,
Ere he shall discover
In the whole wide world again
Such a constant lover.

Such verse is an elegant, and, importantly, an aristocratic form. It insists on, among other things, an exactness of rhyme: *moon* and *June* rather than *moon* and *fan* or *fun*. It has often been observed that rock n roll put "everybody" (Berlin, Porter, Gershwin, etc.) out of business. The roots of rock n roll are folk song and the blues—forms in which exact rhyming is rarely observed and which appear to be far more demotic than the extremely interesting, often complex but implicitly aristocratic lyrics of Gershwin and Hart. One of Porter's most famous lines is *"Fly*ing too *high* with some *guy* in the *sky* is my *i-* / dea...of—nothing to do." The build-up of five rhymes and then the sudden drop. That kind of effect would have little place in a rock n roll song. Bob Dylan's lyrics are nothing like that—which was one of the reasons people decided to call them "poetry." Dylan's brilliant work is rooted in folk songs, blues, in a kind of "light" surrealism, and of course in Beat poetry. But there is another influence there as well. Dylan talks about it in his memoir, *Chronicles, Volume 1*. He used to go to the Theatre de Lys to see the then current production of *Threepenny Opera*. The translation of Brecht's lyrics by Mark Blitzstein was in the folk song tradition—not in the tradition of Porter, Hart:

You people can watch while I'm scrubbing these floors
And I'm scrubbin' the floors while you're gawking
Maybe once ya tip me and it makes ya feel swell
In this crummy Southern town
In this crummy old hotel
But you'll never guess to who you're talkin.'
No. You couldn't ever guess to who you're talkin.'
Then one night there's a scream in the night
And you'll wonder who could that have been
And you see me kinda grinnin' while I'm scrubbin'
And you say, "What's she got to grin?"
I'll tell you.
There's a ship
The Black Freighter
With a skull on its masthead
Will be coming in

Dylan tells of his fascination with Brecht's "Pirate Jenny" song as it was sung by Lotte Lenya. (Indeed, Lenya as Pirate Jenny appears on the cover of Dylan's 1965 LP, *Bringing It All Back Home*.) A sense of apocalypse and implied revolution is very strong in that song. Obviously, for the Communist Brecht, Jenny's fantasy suggests an uprising of the proletariat. Dylan took the sense of apocalypse and implied revolution from "Pirate Jenny," but he left behind the notion of the proletariat: that is, he changed the political focus of the song while keeping much of its revolutionary energy. His 60s songs are all about imminent apocalypse and revolution ("You know that something's happening but you don't know what it is, do you Mr. Jones?"), but they are not about the proletariat. The revolutionaries addressed in his songs were likely to be young, white and bourgeois.

But Bob Dylan was far from being the only one. The aristocratic tradition of elegant, carefully-honed lyrics of Gershwin, Hart and company was swept aside as mainstream music looked not towards "light verse" but towards the kinds of words that people like Alan Lomax and Carl Sandburg had carefully unearthed in their presentations of "folk music." The world of "standards" is implicitly and constantly the world of the *haut-monde*. The world of rock n roll is the world of the down and out. Class issues arose as the young bourgeoisie began to see itself as more like the impecunious than like the well heeled. Porter's attempt to "co-opt" rock n roll, "The Ritz Roll and Rock," is interesting, pathetic and unsuccessful. The song is danced by the great Fred Astaire, who had requested such a number—but it is an *old* Fred Astaire (*Silk Stockings*, 1957; Astaire was 58):

The Rock and Roll is dead and gone

Since the smart set took it on
Because they found it much too tame
They jazzed it up and changed its name

And all they do around the clock
Is the Ritz Roll and Rock...

These fancy fops and fillies
Throw swell affairs
And make those hick hillbillies
Look like squares
It's been at least a year, they say
Since any of them hit the hay

And all they do around the clock
Is the Ritz Roll and Rock

The Porter who announced that "They have found that the fountain of youth / Is a mixture of gin and vermouth" ("Two Little Babes in the Wood") or who, in 1941, used the word "gay" to mean "homosexual" ("Farming"—Danny Kaye sings it with The Fairy Pipers) or who coined the word "tinpantithesis" ("It's De-Lovely") is nowhere to be found in that lyric.

By allying itself to folk song, rock n roll shifted from being a music for teenagers to being a new and extremely interesting music for adults. But when that happened, the notion of what constituted "rhyme" in a popular song was drastically changed:

> Oh, what did you see, my blue eyed son?
> And what did you see, my darling young one?

> I saw a newborn baby with wild wolves all around it
> I saw a highway of diamonds with nobody on it
> I saw a black branch with blood that kept drippin'
> I saw a room full of men with their hammers a-bleedin'
> I saw a white ladder all covered with water
> I saw ten thousand talkers whose tongues were all broken
> I saw guns and sharp swords in the hands of young children
> And it's a hard, it's a hard, it's a hard, and it's a hard
> It's a hard rain's a-gonna fall.

There is a tradition in American popular music that goes back not to the blues or to gospel but to a kind of minstrel-show version of African Americans: the "coon" song, a song whose protagonist is supposedly a black man singing in dialect. In their earliest manifestations, such songs were sung by white singers in blackface. One finds examples in Stephen Foster ("De Camptown Races"), George M. Cohan ("I Guess I'll Have to Telegraph Ma Baby"), Irving Berlin ("Steppin' Out With Ma Baby"), Johnny Mercer ("Ac-Cent-Tchu-Ate the Positive"), Hoagie Carmichael ("Lazy Bones"), Oscar Hammerstein ("Old Man River"), Ira Gershwin ("It Ain't Necessarily So"), and many others. In these songs, the purported "black man" was often comic and full of malapropisms but he could also be a sort of wisdom figure, a truth teller. (He is that in his manifestation as the monologist "Lord Buckley" or in the figure of Uncle Remus in Joel Chandler Harris's tales.) An interesting aspect of Dylan's persona is that, though definitely "folk," *he isn't black*. He is perhaps an old Appalachian man, a singer, a guitar player, a bluesman—and a

Christian. But what he says and sings is in a way a transformation of the coon song. The singer is definitely *related* to African Americans, but he is, importantly, like Elvis Presley, a white man who can "do it too."

There are many influences on Bob Dylan's lyrics—including the "light" surrealism previously mentioned. (The poet Ted Joans liked to point out that surrealism of a sort was a major feature of Southern black speech: one of his favorite examples was "Well, shut my mouth wide open.") The protagonist of Bob Dylan's songs, their speaker—their "inspiration"—is clearly not Robert Allen Zimmerman and the world a man with such a name might inhabit. He is not even "Dylan" Thomas, the source of Bob Dylan's pseudonym. He is a white man, probably an older white man, with considerable experience of the world. Though his twang shows that he is clearly *not* a member of the bourgeoisie or of the college-educated classes, he seems—though a totally fictional creation—*authentic*. If he is often a wisdom figure, he is also to some degree Norman Mailer's "White Negro." He can say highly "poetic" things like this:

With your sheet-metal memory of Cannery Row,
And your magazine-husband who one day just had to go,
And your gentleness now, which you just can't help but show,
Who among them do you think would employ you?
Now you stand with your thief, you're on his parole
With your holy medallion which your fingertips fold,

And your saintlike face and your ghostlike soul,
Oh, who among them do you think could destroy you?

Sad-eyed lady of the lowlands,
Where the sad-eyed prophet says that no man
Comes,
My warehouse eyes, my Arabian drums,
Should I leave them by your gate,
Or, sad-eyed lady, should I wait?

Or this:

Mama, take this badge off of me
I can't use it anymore
It's gettin' dark, too dark to see
I feel like I'm knockin' on heaven's door
Knock, knock, knockin' on heaven's door
Knock, knock, knockin' on heaven's door
Knock, knock, knockin' on heaven's door
Knock, knock, knockin' on heaven's door
Mama, put my guns in the ground
I can't shoot them anymore
That long black cloud is comin' down
I feel like I'm knockin' on heaven's door

Like "It's a Hard Rain," the second passage echoes the ancient
ballad, "Lord Randall," though the context is here transferred to
the American West. Would anyone deny that these words are
poetry? But then, so are these, by Cole Porter:

I should like you all to know,
I'm a famous gigolo.
And of lavender, my nature's got just a dash in it.

As I'm slightly undersexed,
You will always find me next
To some dowager who's wealthy rather than passionate.
Go to one of those night club places
And you'll find me stretching my braces
Pushing ladies with lifted faces
'Round the floor.
But I must confess to you
There are moments when I'm blue.
And I ask myself whatever I do
It for.

I'm a flower that blooms in the winter,
Sinking deeper and deeper in "snow."   [cocaine]
I'm a baby who has
No mother but jazz,
I'm a gigolo.
Ev'ry morning, when labor is over,
To my sweet-scented lodgings I go,
Take the glass from the shelf
And look at myself,
I'm a gigolo.
I get stocks and bonds
From faded blondes
Ev'ry twenty-fifth of December.
Still I'm just a pet
That men forget
And only tailors remember.
Yet when I see the way all the ladies
Treat their husbands who put up the dough,
You cannot think me odd
If then *I thank God*
I'm a gigolo.

．

In the still of the night

As I gaze from my window
At the moon in its flight
My thoughts all stray to you

In the still of the night
While the world is in slumber
Oh, the times without number,
Darling, when I say to you,

Do you love me
As I love you?
Are you my life to be,
My dream come true?

Or will this dream of mine fade out of sight
Like the Moon growing dim
On the rim
Of the hill
In the chill
Still
Of the night?

Do we need to choose between these different modes of poetry? In

the sixties many people felt that we did.

*

ALONG CAME ZIMMERMAN
a song lyric with music provided by my San José friend, Tony
Perez

I gave my heart to Irving Berlin
Gershwin and Rodgers made my head spin

Hammerstein, Kern, Herman Hupfeld too
And also the fellow who wrote "Am I Blue"
But along came Zimmerman
Along came Zimmerman
With his folk guitar and his nasal voice
I gave them all up, I had no choice
He made them all seem passé

I loved Larry Hart so witty was he
And Porter's "beguine" never ended with me
Nobody's higher than Lerner and Lowe
And Loesser's not lesser I'd like you to know
But along came Zimmerman
Along came Zimmerman
With his electric and Joan Baez
And the things he sang that everyone says—
He made them all seem passé

"In olden days a glimpse of stocking"—
That all fell away when he started rocking
We saw revolution in every song
We saw a new world as we sang along
We gasped as he grinned and rang and moaned
We knew Everybody Must Get Stoned

Now, if the creek don't rise and the good Lord's willin'
We'll have a hundred years of that man, Bob Dylan
A hundred years, though at times he's been booed,
A hundred years of his "attitude"
But along came Zimmerman
Along came Zimmerman
With his harmonica and his tongue so tart
And his cocky manner and his stealing heart
He made them seem
Like an old-fashioned dream—
He made them seem passé.

*

DAVID MELTZER IN A LETTER TO ME:

Shadow fighters. *Figuren.*

I proselytized (evangelized) Dylan's first 2 LPs to McClure months before the famous shoot Larry Keenan wrought. McClure was immensely unimpressed & disdainful. Being a working musician in the folk scene then—as well as working as a bookstore clerk at Discovery Books, as well as being a poet, a husband, a father, & febrile & young & ongoing—I "got" the traditional radicality & reality of Dylan as a major singer/songwriter. When we met during his first SF appearance, he reiterated that the "poets had it" & that he was a songwriter, a position he holds to this day, though nobody takes him "seriously." He took poets seriously even while toying w/ Allen like a cat w/ a brilliant mouse. In fact, McClure, Ferlinghetti, to name names, jumped on the rock-star limo because, like Allen, they wanted to be stars. A big mistake; they both had tin ears not unlike Allen who initially was rhythm impaired & somewhat tone-deaf. (Had to accompany him in Allendale, Michigan at some concert hall event & it was hell.)

But those were the days, my friends.

Time for my Ovaltine.

[JACK: One might add here that Michael McClure told me that, hearing him attempting to be a rock star, many of his friends told him, "Michael, don't sing." McClure heeded their advice. After their meeting, Bob Dylan gave McClure a harmonica—a Zimmerman.]

*

FROM "IRVING BERLIN: BIGOTRY AND BRILLIANCE": some speculations on one of the great American songwriters (lyrics AND music)

If we leave out the extremely significant contributions of African-American songwriters to popular music, certainly the next most prolific and successful group would have to be Jews: Berlin, Gershwin, Kern, Rodgers, Bernstein, etc. It's interesting to note that not a single one of these Jewish songwriters ever wrote a love song to a Jewish woman. Though Berlin wrote "Marie from Sunny Italy," there was no "Rachel from Jerusalem" (or in Berlin's case, more likely "Sonia from Russia") to vie with Marie. Irish composers, on the other hand—including Berlin's idol, George M. Cohan—wrote many songs about the erotic virtues of Irish women, and there were certainly songs written by black composers about black women. Ellington's "Tall, Tan, and Terrific" is one example. Jewish assimilation dictated that comedians such as Eddie Cantor could be explicitly Jewish—but their love interests could not.

When Jewish women appear in popular songs they are figures of fun—"Second Hand Rose" or Berlin's own "Sadie Salome, Go Home" (1909): "Most ev'rybody knows / That I'm your loving Mose, / Oy, oy, oy, oy, / Where is your clothes?" We're not far here from the great African-American singer-composer, Shelton Brooks: "I'll lend you everything I've got except for my wife, / And I'll make you a present of her"—a 1910 song written by Jean C. Havez and Harry Von Tilzer and popularized by the great black comedian, Bert Williams, whom Brooks imitated. In effect, the American Irish, not likely to return to the "ould sod," were trying not only to combat "No Irish Need Apply" but to be *more Irish* than they were; the American Jews were trying to be *less Jewish* than they were: though their audience was Jewish and they played to them, they also knew that there was in America an undercurrent of hatred of the Jews.

But if we are looking for bigotry *within* Irving Berlin's work, we don't have far to go. Irving Berlin was a brilliant, complex, sometimes bigoted songwriter who produced, in addition to some of the most memorable songs ever produced by an American, a plethora of "coon songs" and minstrel numbers, including the famous "Alexander's Ragtime Band"—songs that appeared less racist in the context of the times perhaps but were racist nonetheless. The "America" that arises from his work recalls that of Alexis de Tocqueville, whose *Democracy in America* appeared in the original French and then in English translation between 1835 and 1840. In America, writes de Tocqueville, "Continual changes are...every instant occurring under the observation of every man"; there is "universal tumult," an "incessant conflict of jarring interests"; "everyone is in motion." De Tocqueville's words were astonishingly prophetic. Universal tumult, jarring interests, Capitalism, cities, the body's need to express itself in a situation in which it is increasingly denied by metropolitan forces are all in the music that Berlin and Gershwin and many others (including African Americans like James T. Brymn—sometimes billed as "Mr. Jazz Himself"—Fats Waller, and Duke Ellington) created a hundred years after de Tocqueville published his book.

Irving Berlin's ballads reach back to different roots from his syncopated, jazz-oriented pieces—to Stephen Foster, for example. But even in Foster's distortions of African-American experience— was there ever any African American who said anything like "D Camptown ladies sing dis song, doodah, doodah?"—the plaintiveness of African-American spirituals and blues have their say: "We will sing one song for my old Kentucky home...." Isn't that song an ancestor of "White Christmas," a ballad which echoes sentimental reminiscences of "d old plantation?" "White Christmas" is anything but a "coon song"—the verse makes clear that it takes place "in Beverley Hills, LA"!—but its sentimental invocation of "home" is not unlike those songs that located "home" in a fictional Old South. I sometimes think that without self-pity we couldn't have popular songs. Irving Berlin's ballads are marvelous examples of self-pity transformed into sound—"said" as music. Is "White Christmas" a sort of white blues? Are the "blues" in Berlin's "Blue Skies" a sort of positive answer to the great African-American genre?

How could Irving Berlin—Israel Isidore Bellin, a Jew born in Imperial Russia in 1888—write a song about the great Christian holiday, Christmas? Berlin wrote "White Christmas" in 1940, and he did with it what he had done in 1933 with another central Christian holiday, Easter. He *secularized* it. Easter is a holiday announcing Christ's resurrection. Christians celebrate it by going to church. Berlin's song, "Easter Parade," doesn't mention Christ, doesn't mention resurrection, doesn't even mention church— though the people "parading" in the song are going there. Similarly, if Christmas is a celebration of the birth of Christ, "White Christmas" doesn't say anything about that. It is a nostalgic image of an idealized holiday which perhaps never really existed. It's like the films about a typical America made by Jewish filmmakers. Did the America of Andy Hardy ever really exist? It's an America dreamed by people who were in many ways outsiders, exiles—immigrants—but who, like Berlin, were immensely successful in America. "White Christmas" accurately calls itself a "dream."

...

Another Jewish composer, Kurt Weill—an immigrant from Nazi Germany—faced the implications of the secularization of Christianity far more clearly than Irving Berlin. These lyrics, written by Maxwell Anderson, were sung by a black preacher in the musical play, *Lost in the Stars*, produced on Broadway in 1949. *Lost in the Stars* was Kurt Weill's last show. This is the title song. The lyrics are excellent, but it is the music that carries the weight of the cosmic desolation that is the ultimate result of secularization. Pascal: "The eternal silence of these infinite spaces frightens me." The show is based on Alan Paton's book, *Cry the Beloved Country*. For Weill, the "beloved country" was not an idealized secular version of a Christian holiday but may well have conjured up not only South Africa, the subject of Paton's book, but his native Germany, the country he had been forced to leave. In the original production, the song was sung by Todd Duncan, who had played Porgy in the original production of Gershwin's *Porgy and Bess* (1935). As in *Porgy and Bess*—as in "White Christmas"—the lyrics carry just a hint of the minstrel show even as they attempt to move well beyond it.

Before Lord God made the Sea and the Land
He held all the stars in the palm of his hand
And they ran through his fingers like grains of sand
And one little star fell alone

Then the Lord God hunted through the wide night air
For the little dark star on the wind down there
And he stated and promised He'd take special care
So it wouldn't get lost again

Now a man don't mind if the stars grow dim
And the clouds blow over and darken him
So long as the Lord God's watching over them
Keeping track how it all goes on—

But I've been walking through the night and the day
Till my eyes get weary and my head turns grey
And sometimes it seems maybe God's gone away
Forgetting His promise that we heard him say
And we're lost out here in the stars

Little stars, big stars
Blowing through the night...

And we're lost out here in the stars
Little stars, big stars
Blowing through the night...

(CHORUS)
And we're lost
And we're lost
And we're lost
And we're lost

(SOLOIST)
And we're lost
Out here in the stars

"Home" is, precisely, a space in which we are not "lost." Berlin
was an immigrant, and an immigrant may be defined as a person

caught between two "homes." His songs are a magnificent attempt to bridge the gap between ancient Russia (and all that meant) and the USA. As a child he witnessed his first "home" (in Russia) totally destroyed in a pogrom. "White Christmas" conjures a new home, as does Berlin's "God Bless America": "my home sweet home." The latter song was suggested as a replacement for our hard-to-sing national anthem. It's said that Berlin's song would have been refused because Berlin was Jewish. Irving Berlin came to America as a child and was a great success at "writing its popular songs." But he learned as well that there were certain lines that he as a Jew could not cross. He gave America dreams, including its dream of the fake "Negro," the minstrel, and of a totally secularized holy day, but if in a way he was a sterling example of the American Dream, he was also subject to the bigotry at the heart of American entertainment: he was a Jew and a Jew— no matter what he wrote, no matter how much money he made— was never, even at Christmas, "white."

*

SEA BREEZE

BRISE MARINE

La chair est triste, hélas! et j'ai lu tous les livres.
Fuir! là-bas fuir! Je sens que des oiseaux sont ivres
D'être parmi l'écume inconnue et les cieux!

Rien, ni les vieux jardins reflétés par les yeux
Ne retiendra ce coeur qui dans la mer se trempe
Ô nuits! ni la clarté déserte de ma lampe
Sur le vide papier que la blancheur défend,
Et ni la jeune femme allaitant son enfant.
Je partirai! Steamer balancant ta mâture,
Lève l'ancre pour une exotique nature!
Un Ennui, désolé par les cruels espoirs,
Croit encore à l'adieu suprême des mouchoirs!
Et, peut-être, les mâts, invitant les orages
Sont-ils de ceux qu'un vent penche sur les naufrages
Perdus, sans mâts, sans mâts, ni fertiles îlots...
Mais, ô mon coeur, entends le chant des matelots!
    —Stéphane Mallarmé (1865)

In "Crise de vers" (1896) Mallarmé writes, "L'oeuvre pure implique la disparition élocutoire du poète, qui cède l'initiative aux mots...." ("The pure work implies the disappearance of the poet as speaker, yielding his initiative to words....")

...

A century ago in Paris, the painter Degas had lamented that his poems weren't any good though his ideas were wonderful, and the poet Mallarmé responded, "But my dear Degas, poems are made of words, not ideas."

http://www.modernamericanpoetry.org/category/tags/degas

Mallarmé's commentators seem not to have noticed the extraordinary pun at the conclusion of "Brise Marine." In the poem's penultimate line, everything is lost ("Perdus"): there are no masts ("mâts") and no isles ("îlots")—they have vanished: "Perdus, sans mâts, sans mâts, ni fertiles îlots..." Yet, in a sense, the concluding word, "matelots," *gives the poet back* the very things he has lost: the *sound* of "matelots" ("sailors") contains "mâts" + "îlots." The "lost" masts and isles are not restored to the poet as entities, only as names, echoing words. *But that is all they were to begin with.* In a way, the proper translation of the concluding line is "But, oh my heart, listen to the song of 'mâts' + 'îlots.'" One can sense in this early poem—written when the author was in his twenties—an extraordinary shift from a focus on "things" to a focus on "words." The poem insists that it is not a description of reality, not even of imagined reality: rather, it is something made out of words, and if you lose something in the context of words—as opposed to the context of reality—then it can be restored through words. If, from one point of view, the poet's fear of action—of actually making the trip announced by the poem—propels him to find refuge in language, from another point of view the poem enunciates a new mode of beauty. How far are we here from the strategies of *Finnegans Wake*? My translation attempts to include the pun and to include it on the same word as the French: sail/oars-sailors. Note also that Mallarmé's penultimate line is only eleven syllables, not twelve. The ... is the twelfth syllable.

SEA BREEZE

The flesh is sad, alas! and I've read all the books.
To run away—to run away *down there*. I feel that birds are drunk
They want to be in unknown foam and skies!
Nothing—not even the gardens reflected in your eyes—
Will hold this heart that drenches in the sea—
Ah, nights!—not even the desolate brilliance of the lamp by which I see
The virginal paper whose white-
Ness defends it, nor the young wife
With child suckling: I'm leaving—
Weigh anchor!—going to a place where there is no grieving.
An immense Boredom—thrust from hope to griefs—
Believes still in the supreme goodbye of waving handkerchiefs!...

—And perhaps the masts will summon storms
That blast the sails and wreck the oars:
Lost, without sail, without sail, or beating oars...

But oh, my heart, listen to the song of *sailors*.

*

FROM *ALL: A JAMES BROUGHTON READER* / POETRY & FILM

When Shelley began his great poem, "Epipsychidion" with "My Song, I fear that thou wilt find but few / Who fitly shall conceive thy reasoning," or when Yeats began his *Collected Poems* with "The Song of the Happy Shepherd," neither poet expected the reader to take the word "song" too literally. (In fact, both poets expected the reader to recognize that they were alluding to certain *books*—in Yeats's case, Blake's *"Songs" of Innocence and Experience* and in Shelley's, Dante's *Convito*.) In their works the word "song" was for the most part a literary convention. The primary way of disseminating poetry for these poets was not—as it was for Homer—the mouth, the sound of the poet's voice, but the page. And the page is taken in, not with the ears, as a "song" is, but with the eyes.

Still, neither Shelley nor Yeats takes very much advantage of that fact: neither of them uses the page to any significant extent, not even to the extent that James Broughton uses the page in his poetry. For them, the white space of the page is essentially neutral. This was not, however, the case for Stéphane Mallarmé when, in 1897, he published *Un coup de dés jamais n'abolira le hasard* (*A Throw of the Dice Will Never Abolish Chance*), a poem in which the silence and whiteness of the page is anything but neutral.

Un coup de dés marks the very first moment in which a modern poet *admits* that he is working with a page and that the page itself, even the entire book, can be used for expressive purposes. One of the terms Mallarmé uses to designate the page is *toile*, which means, among other things, "sail"—like the page, white—and "canvas," what a painter uses for his art. Beginning with that poem, modern poetry embarks upon an enormously important experiment, an experiment which continues into the present day. It is an experiment with *specifically visual experience*. Mallarmé not only accepts the silence and whiteness of the page as the primary means for the dissemination of his poetry; he makes active use of it.

This is not the place to enter into the historical ramifications of *Un coup de dés*, but suffice it to say that that poem gives birth to an extraordinary series of experiments with typefaces, with white space, with patterns, with letters (as in Apollinaire and E. E. Cummings), with "field" techniques (as in Charles Olson), with all sorts of *essentially visual phenomena*. In addition, poets begin to claim that their work is *grounded* in the visual, in "images," and for the first time it is possible to argue—as C. Day Lewis does in *The Poetic Image* (1947)—that "imagery," not what Homer called "the power of harmony," is the very basis of poetry.

The connection of all this to the films of James Broughton is perhaps already clear. Broughton is one of the few significant modern poets to have taken the concern with "imagery" to one of its possible conclusions. *The whiteness of the page becomes in his work the whiteness of the screen, which Broughton "fills" with "images" of all sorts.* Indeed, he is able to go even further than that. By adding a soundtrack to his films he is able to give poetry back precisely what the page took from it: the sound of the poet's voice.

His films are thus fascinating responses to a problem central to all modern literature. What we call "writing" is traditionally grounded in speech, in the aural/oral, yet it depends for its dissemination not on the aural but on the visual, on the page. Broughton's films raise the question of whether there are not—as indeed there seem to be—alternative ways of presenting "writing."

*

FROM "WORDS & BOOKS; POETRY & WRITING"
The complete essay is published in my book, *O Powerful Western Star* (2000). It is performed by Adelle and me on the CD accompanying the book.

Is the poet public or is he private? Do his words move outward to the world or inward towards a pure subjectivity, an "essence of words"? Are both these stances myths—and, if they are, what are they expressing? What do they have to do with *Wen Fu*, "the art of writing"?

Writing about writing in his great book, *Interfaces of the Word*, Father Walter J. Ong refers to "the indissoluble alliance which writing and print have with death, the great separator." Writing turns "performer" and "listener," who are necessarily physically present to one another, into "author" and "reader," who are necessarily not. Writer and reader are separated—as if by death:

"Even by Jane Austen's time...the problem of the reader's role in prose narrative was by no means entirely solved. Nervousness regarding the role of the reader registers everywhere in the 'dear reader' regularly invoked in fiction well through the nineteenth century. The reader had to be reminded (and the narrator, too) that the recipient of the story was indeed a reader—not a listener, not one of the crowd, but an individual isolated with a text."

"Not a listener, not one of the crowd, but an individual isolated with a text." The isolation of Lu Chi's poet in *Wen Fu* is indeed linked to "the art of writing." Writing for both writer and reader tends towards isolation—towards separateness, towards "privacy." I need to be alone so I can write. I need to get away in order to finish my novel. The image of Lu Chi's poet is the image, by now enormously hackneyed, of the sensitive, isolated, perhaps even "misunderstood" individual—a figure whose isolation mirrors the isolation of the reader alone with his book. The reader's eyes are not in fact closed, as the poet's are, but they are nevertheless turned away from the world. They are focused on a *book*, not on the world around him.

In the mirror of his text, Lu Chi's words apply as much to the reader as they do to the poet:

"Eyes closed, he hears an inner music; he is lost in thoughts and questions—
His spirit rides to the eight corners of the universe, his mind a thousand miles away."

The figure of the heroic poet listening to "an inner music" is a mythologizing of the act of reading. What has reading to do with poetry? What happens when, as Eric A. Havelock puts it, "the muse learns to write"? The Homeric poet's blindness is an indication that he has nothing at all to do with writing. There was no Braille in Homer's day. At its beginnings, poetry is rooted in physical presence and in sounds, and, whatever the labyrinthine complexities of its history—and they are many—it always maintains some sort of connection with its purely oral past. "In a shell of murmurings," wrote Robert Duncan in the 1960s,

> rimed round,
> sound-chamberd child
> (*Bending the Bow*)

"Well then," said Socrates to Phaedrus,

are we able to imagine another sort of discourse, a legitimate brother of our bastard [writing]? How does it originate? How far is it better and more powerful in nature?

Phaedrus. What sort of discourse? What do you mean about its origin?

Socrates. A discourse which is inscribed with genuine knowledge in the soul of the learner; a discourse that can defend itself and knows to whom it should speak and before whom to remain silent.

Phaedrus. Do you mean the living, animate discourse of a man who really knows? Would it be fair to call the written discourse only a kind of ghost of it?

Socrates. Precisely.

—Plato, *The Phaedrus*

Written discourse, writes Plato, is "only a kind of ghost" of "the living, animate discourse of a man who really knows."

The shift from Socrates, who never wrote anything, to Plato, who was a writer, is the shift from an oral culture to a culture in which writing is of enormous importance. It is the beginning of the myth of subjectivity, of inwardness, a myth which finds its apotheosis in the conception of the "unconscious," a conception of an area of the mind so "subjective" that it is for the most part inaccessible. The history of this myth of subjectivity is bound up with the history of writing. Do we speak our words aloud as we write or read them or are we silent before the page? Just as there are areas of the mind which must be "read," "interpreted," "decoded" before they can be understood, so words—the products of our breaths and bodies—are hidden in the tangles of "letters."

The following poem, published by E. E. Cummings in 1935 in his volume, *No Thanks*, is, literally, unspeakable:

r-p-o-p-h-e-s-s-a-g-r
            who
a)s w(e loo)k
upnowgath
        PPEGORHRASS
                        eringint(o-
aThe) :l
        eA
            !p:
S   a
            (r
rIvInG   .gRrEaPsPhOs)
                                        to
rea(be)rran(com)gi(e)ngly
,grasshopper;

                            [Speakers are silent while
                            audience examines poem]

Cummings' poem brilliantly places us at the exact point at which letters turn into words. The struggle to see the grasshopper as it moves and leaps in the grass is mirrored by the struggle of our eyes to make sense—and words—out of Cummings' disarranged letters. But it is an entirely *visual* struggle. R-p-o-p-h-e-s-s-a-g-r cannot be pronounced except as individual letters until one turns the letters around and perceives them to be "grasshopper." It is as far from the oral as a poem can be.

At a certain point in its history, Western poetry takes the page, and "letters," as its primary mode of dissemination. The ancestor of Cummings' poem is Stéphane Mallarmé's *Un coup de dés, A Throw of the Dice Will Never Abolish Chance*, a poem published in 1897. Mallarmé's poem marks the very first moment in which a modern poet *admits* that he is working with a page and that the page, even the entire book, can be used for expressive purposes. Beginning with that poem (which, Mallarmé says, "has no precedent") modern poetry embarks upon an enormously important experiment, an experiment which continues into the present day: an experiment with *specifically visual experience*. Mallarmé not only *accepts* the silence and whiteness of the page as the primary means for the dissemination of his poetry, he makes active use of it.

I cannot possibly enter into the historical ramifications of *Un coup de dés* but suffice it to say that that poem gives birth to an extraordinary series of experiments with typefaces, with white space, with patterns, with letters (in Apollinaire as well as E. E. Cummings), with "field" techniques (as in Charles Olson), with all sorts of *essentially visual phenomena*. In addition, poets begin to claim that their work is *grounded* in the visual, in "images," and for the first time it is possible to argue, as C. Day Lewis does in *The Poetic Image* (1947), that "imagery," not what Homer calls the "power of harmony," is the very basis of poetry. The intense visual focus on the book, which is necessary if reading is to occur at all, becomes the very theme and condition of poetry. The poem exists, as Cummings puts it very well, only "a)s w(e loo)k."

Yet this is by no means the end of the story. Writing is itself at this moment in *a state of crisis.* For the first time in its history it finds itself *in competition* with other modes of expression. Our children, we complain, don't read enough. Literacy is declining. For many years writing was the only way of preserving human speech—but this is no longer the case. The cassette tape or the phonograph record or the radio or the television or the CD can give you the exact sound of the person who is speaking.

In his book *The Muse Learns To Write*, Eric A. Havelock reflects upon the new interest in orality which has characterized much scholarship in the past twenty-five to thirty years. Why, he asks, "should...works produced simultaneously in three different countries have all involved themselves in the role of human language in human culture? Why, in particular, this focus on the spoken language in contrast to the written?" His answer is: *"We had all been listening to the radio..."* (my italics).

The electronic media have already changed the conditions of writing, though the exact nature of that change is not yet clear. We live, as Father Ong put it in 1977, in an "opening state of consciousness," a state in which even the nature of biography—the nature of what we believe it means to be human—may have to be reconsidered.

Lu Chi's inward-looking poet, the type of the subjective man, may strike us as oddly old-fashioned. The figure of the Homeric singer, with its very different sense of personality structure, has been a haunting presence in modern literature, whether one speaks of James Joyce or W. B. Yeats or H. D. or Ezra Pound or Jack Kerouac or Judy Grahn. What are we likely to experience next? We don't know, but we have an intense sense that it is likely to be *different*.

...

This passage is also from *O Powerful Western Star*. I delivered it as part of "The Performance Poetry Bash" at Fort Mason, San Francisco, for Herman Berlandt's National Poetry Week II (San Francisco, 1988):

> Camerado, this is no book...
> —Walt Whitman, "So Long"

Performance poetry is an active and intellectually engaged response to the silence and whiteness in which most poetry remains entangled. Writing of Mallarmé, Frederick R. Karl remarked, "The page or territory is primary, on which language wanders like a lonely adventurer hoping to survive emptiness and whiteness." The performance poet insists that s/he is not a mere adjunct of a book but rather a manifestation of what books arise out of: the physical presence of the author. Historically, "poetry" and "writing" remain in a state of tension. (Homer was a poet, not a writer.) Performance poetry seeks to tilt that tension in the direction of presence, to insist on the limitations of writing as a medium for the presentation of the art. At the heart of writing, at the heart of all mass culture, is a profound and disturbing absence. Performance poetry is an insistence that absence, silence and whiteness—the page—are not the only conditions in which poetry can be "heard."

*

STEPHEN COLE ASKED ME ABOUT YEATS...
a short essay on W.B.Y.

There is much to be said. I've written (and published) a couple of papers about Yeats, one of my master poets. I believe that the "official" interpretations of several of his poems are inaccurate. "Among School Children" and "The Second Coming" are spectacularly so. Yeats was an ESOTERIC poet: there are things you need to know when you encounter his poems.

As Paul de Man was the first to notice, shining through Yeats' naturalistic "imagery" is a notion expounded by the Neoplatonist, Porphyry (232/3 - ca. 305) in his *De Antro Nympharum*, a commentary on the Cave of the Nymphs episode in *The Odyssey*. Yeats knew Porphyry's essay through Thomas Taylor's widely-read translation, and he refers explicitly to it in the footnote about "the drug" in "Among School Children." He quotes extensively from the essay in "The Philosophy of Shelley's Poetry"—one of the essays collected in *Ideas of Good and Evil* (1903)—and there are unmistakable references to Porphyry in both Blake and Spenser as well as in Yeats' own work. Appearing in *The Witch of Atlas*, *The Book of Thel*, and in the third Book of *The Faerie Queene*, the cluster of symbols discussed in Porphyry's essay is one of the key items of literary Neo-Platonism.

As described by Porphyry, the Cave of the Nymphs is a kind of half-way house for all souls about to be born or about to ascend to heaven; as such it is regarded as the source of all life, which is symbolized by "waters welling everywhere." One of its gates—"the gate of generation"—leads to the earth, and the other—"the gate of ascent through death to the gods"—leads to heaven. The first is "the gate of cold and moisture"—for "cold...causes life in the world"—and the second is "the gate of heat and fire." If we keep only these details in mind—and Porphyry goes on to add a great many others—we can see how the Cave of the Nymphs is relevant to a poem such as "The Wild Swans at Coole." The "brimming water among the stones," for example, is Yeats' equivalent to the water welling among the rocks of the cave, and

the two activities of the swans—"They paddle in the cold /
Companionable streams or climb the air"—represent respectively
the descent of the soul into matter through the gate of cold and
moisture and, since air is a purer element than water, the ascent to
the divine. Yeats often imagines this ascent as proceeding in
"rings" or "gyres" and as accompanied by the sound of a bell—
here, "the bell-beat of their wings above my head." (Cf. the bells in
"Byzantium" and "All Souls' Night.")

There are many implications to Porphyry in Yeats. And it is
important to know that the two gates are always a unitary
phenomenon: where the one gate is the other is as well: "They
paddle in the cold / Companionable streams or climb the air."

Many of Yeats' poems change their meanings once we allow for
the presence of Porphyry and other esoteric elements. I mentioned
that the two gates are a unitary phenomenon. In a poem like "The
Second Coming," the entire opening passage is usually taken to
mean more or less the same thing. From memory:

Turning and turning in the widening gyre,
The falcon cannot hear the falconer.
Things fall apart; the center cannot hold.
Mere anarchy is loosed upon the world,
etc.

The falcon's inability to hear the falconer is parallel to things
falling apart, another example of "anarchy": an image of chaos.

Perhaps.

But note the concluding lines: "And what rough beast, its hour come round at last / Slouches towards Bethlehem to be born?" Being born: that's the gate of generation. Where then is the other gate, "the gate of ascent"?

Turning and turning in the widening gyre,
The falcon cannot hear the falconer.

The opening lines are *not* an image of chaos: they are an image of *escape*. The falconer is trying to lure the falcon back to the earth, where everything is falling apart. The falcon is escaping from all that and moving towards the divine: "They paddle in the cold, / Companionable streams *or climb the air*." It is the only moment in the poem where Yeats offers us an alternative to the way of the beast.

That Yeats allows his reader to misunderstand the opening lines is part of why we must regard him as an *esoteric* writer. If you have been through the proper initiation, if you know your Porphyry, you may understand him. For the ordinary reader, the poem is only about the horrors of the modern world.

Similarly, the conclusion of "Among School Children" is pretty much universally taken to be positive—about a state in which you can't tell dancer from dance. The line is understood as a rhetorical question. But the whole burden of the poem is about distinctions, particularly the distinction between images. "Both nuns and mothers worship images, / But those the candle lights are not as those / That animate a mother's reveries." Two diametrically opposed kinds of images. The young Yeats took Maud Gonne's beauty to be an image of divine beauty—an image like those worshipped by nuns. As he looks at her in the now of the poem, she is anything but that: "Her present image floats into the mind, / Did Quattrocento finger fashion it? / Hollow of cheek as though it drank the wind / And took a mess of shadows for its meat." Her growing old is a clear indication that she is the kind of image that animates a mother's reveries. Was his reaction to her the reaction of his soul or was it his libido? The poem is a reluctant and oblique admission that it was the latter. The answer to the first of the concluding questions, "O chestnut tree, great rooted blossomer, / Are you the leaf, the blossom or the bole?," is NO, IT IS NOT. The great rooted blossomer is an image like those that nuns worship; it is not the tree that exists in nature, exists in time: leaf and blossom are temporal phenomena. The second question, "O body swayed to music, O brightening glance, / How can we know the dancer from the dance?" is not a rhetorical question asserting the unity of dancer and dance but a genuine, anguished question. Yeats' failure to know the difference between dancer (nature) and dance (archetypal image) in the case of his misplaced "worship" of Maud Gonne will certainly cost him time in Purgatory (cf. his play on that subject), may in fact cost him his soul.

Commentaries: Random thoughts on the art of poetry
and on a few other things, too
145

I can quote passages in support of what I'm saying here but there isn't room. This should give you an idea. "The Lake Isle of Innisfree" is also misinterpreted—it's full of images straight out of Porphyry—as is "A Dialogue of Self and Soul," which deals with the purgatorial process of living your whole life backwards, not with the possibility of living again, reincarnation. Etc. A central poem in this mode of understanding, a poem which documents the "failure" at the heart of Yeats' enterprise, is "Her Vision in the Wood," which quotes Porphyry's phrase, "fabulous symbol"—a phrase that sums up the young Yeats' hopes for poetry—and admits that what the poet "saw" wasn't a "fabulous symbol" at all but "my heart's victim and its torturer." Misplaced Eros. How can we know the dancer from the dance?

...

Jake Berry and Ray Miller suggested that I write a book on Yeats setting everything straight. I answered,

Taking on the entrenched Yeats industry would be a major undertaking and would require a large, heavily researched book. I remember Thomas Parkinson—a nice, intelligent man who was an early champion of the Beats and who wrote two books about Yeats—saying to me ruefully, "I wish Paul de Man had never written about Yeats." I'm sure he did. The Yeats industry *doesn't want to hear what I have to say*. One professor, F.D. Reeve, ended our friendship when he read my articles. I don't want to spend my declining years doing battle with the Yeats industry. I'd rather write poetry. Paul de Man, who became quite famous and respected, couldn't make a difference. What makes you think I could? You don't understand the strength of the misunderstanding of Yeats. Such an undertaking would involve me in endless battle and endless frustration. Tell your grandchildren about it but don't ask me to write a book about Yeats.

...

To another friend:

You're probably unaware of the Yeats industry. It has published hundreds and hundreds of books and they all say more or less the same thing. There is a lot of time, money, and ego involved in this passionate assertion. If, on the other hand, you pay close attention to Yeats' language and his writing as a whole, these interpretations—commonplace in the understanding of almost everyone who has written or talked about Yeats—fall apart. They are based on early misunderstandings that appeared in the first books about Yeats. What is interesting is the tenacity with which these interpretations are held to even in the face of fairly convincing criticism. Why? What other such interpretations are being held to in the face of facts? James Joyce understood very well that a poem gains life after death through people interpreting an author's work: in fact, Joyce deliberately incorporated riddles for scholars to solve in his work. "I'll give those literary birds something to chirp about for the next hundred years." But what if the interpretations—which give the poet life—are inaccurate? Please don't tell me that everyone interprets texts differently, we're all "individuals." That simply isn't true. If it were true, Madison Avenue would be out of business. The poet's interpreters are important—both for himself and for the wider cultural impact of his work. He is given life through his interpreters. But what if they are wrong? And worse, what if they perpetuate their inaccuracy through a vast network of books, statements, assurances?

W.B.Y.

Gone at 73,
Poet of Ireland
Poet of the Other World
Looking for its traces
In the Wind
Among the Reeds
None like him
For the passion
Of renunciation
"O what a sweetness strayed
To barren Thebaid"
"The foul rag and bone shop
Of the heart"—
Three books
Quote that line
And leave "foul" out—
None like him
For the continual

Recognition
That language
Always goes beyond itself—
Innisfree
Haunted by the words
Of a 3rd-century Neo Platonist—
The immense distance between
This world
And that other
From which
The "voices" came.
Love of the woman
Love of the woman as symbol
The tragedy
That spirit
Lodges itself
In the mire
Of flesh
And that a woman
Must grow old—
Not "unity"
But the fierce knowledge
That all we have
Is the power to know
What we cannot be or emulate.
The swans
Leap up in the pool
And descend again, and leap again.
I love him for the clarity of his monumental, daring, unerring
vision.

.

I have lived with him throughout my life
Lived with the symbols
The magic that leapt about his table
Lived not where he walked

But where he thought
In that sky to which Helena Blavatsky brought him
Demon Est Deus Inversus

.

In the dark you entered in 1939,
Did Plato and Plotinus welcome you?

Did your soul rise, a falcon in the air
Ignoring cries to bring it back to earth?

Did Cúchulainn honor you, show you the sword
That killed in battle frenzy the hound of Culain?

Did Emer soothe the wounds that ended you
And bind them deeply with a purple cloak?

Did honeybees ignore you in that dark
Where wild swans flew and fire sweetly burned?

Did all the gyres end, did darkness sing?
Did you become a consecrated bone?

.

Nothing is true, dear love, nothing is true.

*

POE/LONGFELLOW

Poe
Ruined
Longfellow:

His insistence
That there was
"No such thing
As a long poem."
Longfellow helped his ruination along
With the unfortunate meter
(Skewered by Lewis Carroll)
Of *Hiawatha*.
But *The Courtship of Miles Standish*
And *Evangeline*
Are beautiful poems.
Poe got him, got him in just the way he wished
And we have been paying the price
Ever since.
Poe wrote of Longfellow
With what seems to be astonishing prescience:
"We will grant him certain qualities
But we will deny him
The future."
The short poem rules.

[But cf. "Sweeney Adrift"]

*

FROM *LETTERS*

with a nightmare face
                    foreheadless & chinless
  from the brow ridges
                         in a level line
      juts out like the beak of a bird
                              the septum of the nose
        a complicated tatu in green ink
      principal sites greatly post-dated those of the old

possesses histories
perfoce unsettled fattened on maize are newly fed
a dish to beat
were they the degeneration from
stands with the sacrificial knife
forcibly united
dated inscriptions cease to be carved
lamps to the likeness of a faintly-glowing macaw
they do not know how many days
from a sweaty face, then the body rolled down
ceremonial domestication
what happened to the potato
seed planting of aboriginal
a lot of our native crops
asserted that vision comes from the rays of the eyes
capture, nursing by a foster mother
rightly towards us
but I don't want you
to think
I have ever seen
once every month he used to take some
Latcham in Santiago, who, I found
"The Golden Bough"
when Xenothon celebrated the return to his country he made
great offerings of swine
many times the size those of sorghums
the wild forms live in the mountains well above
Isthus of Panama
culturally there are a number
what seas what shores what grey rocks and what islands
many indecorums in other parts
obstinate peevish willful self-conceited
come closer again
he heth consumed a whole night in lying
raigne, especially
he enjoy a bell for mass
to the Morning Star she gave him all that she had

in quick dance time while the whistle & drum are sounded
the Power of the Flint from the Morning Star
the Power of the Storm
the lion also confirms the attribution
a few human beings have as yet traveled
songs of war/huntingsongs/bartersongs
songs to cure the sick/corn/grinding songs
hand game songs/cradle songs/holy or
"medicine"/songs
league fell apart

*

FOR WILLIAM BLAKE'S BIRTHDAY (NOV. 28)
"nunnes blake" (Geoffrey Chaucer/John Skelton): Blake must have
known the early spelling of "black"

Today's the day of William Blake
Who was also "William Black"
Listen to the little boy
Singing of his bitter lack:

My soul is white, sang William Black
The English boy is white as snow
But I'm the furious jungle beast
Who feasts on everything below

I'm William Black sang William Blake
I am a riddle to your soul
Shall I the Christian God forsake
To make a new bright-shining foal?

For William Black *is* William Blake
I make the fur, the flesh, the shell
I made the Songs of Innocence

And of Experience I tell

I sing of joy I sing of woe
I sing the Everlasting Night
I sing the little jungle boy
Whose soul is dark, bereaved of Light

I'm William Black sang William Blake
I have a warring in my soul
I shall the Christian God forsake
To make a new, bright-shining foal.

*

FOR JOE MASI ON HIS AND EMILY'S BIRTHDAY, DEC. 10

Our lives go by—a loaded gun—
We wonder when the bullet comes—
Eternity is at our side—
How many suns?

We sigh and love and send a gift
To those we wish to hold—
And yet, in Time, we fall bereft
Things tarnish, even gold

To Hospital we go when sick—
The Play has many Acts—
Life passes like arithmetic
It adds—but it subtracts

Love is our governor, he rules
Like Father when we're young—
He whispers, "You've done well, my dear"

And then he whispers, "Come"

*

ON THE DAY OF YOUR BIRTH I HAD A DREAM OF THE DEATH OF POETS
for Jerome Rothenberg on his 89th, December 11, 2020

From 2019:
We cover our animal nature with clothing
And so the animals that we are are not revealed
And we can pretend to be masters of nature, guardians of nature,
The "different" animal.
But at some point in our lives
Nature simply loses interest in us and we "go,"
As all animals "go,"
If we may put it that way. "He go box"
Said Joe Terio, an Italian immigrant (Calabrese), a relative, about many,
And I have just heard of the death of Lyn Lifshin
You have lived long and amply and wonderfully
And stayed true to the only way out of this death trap,
Life: words.
Words are the only immortality we know
And though they are never certain
(Longfellow thought he would be the great poet of his age!)
They are the only certainty we have.
"Words alone are certain good."

.

On the day of your birth I had a dream of the death of poets
Not death but murder as Lorca or Radnóti were murdered
Slaughtered by thugs
And so of the death of poetry

Would we be able to keep
A little notebook in our pockets
That someone would find in the mass grave in which we lay
Soaked with our bodily fluids.
"Der springt noch auf."
His murderer's words immortalized by the poet.

.

On the day of your birth I remembered the deep experience
Of listening to *The Waste Land* with you
As I drove my car who knows where
And you said, "Jesus, Eliot was a great poet."
We knew where we had come from
And we knew that you had extended that clarity
Into new illuminations from all over the world.
"Der springt noch auf."

.

And now, in the full consciousness of your gift,
You give us the masterful *Book of Infernos*:

"the privilege of the rich
escaped & safe

the sky no longer
beckoning

who hide behind
each other

driving back
the dark invaders

they are the final guides

for this inferno

guarding what they build
& plunder

under a black sun
that will lead us

to another world
a gilded hell

the hungry earth
absent a dream

unable to call us
home"

On the day of your birth I remembered what you had done, and laughed at death

*

DISCUSSION WITH A FRIEND

I worked largely in total isolation until I was forty-five, at which point I began to have an audience and to know other poets. By then, most of the issues animating my work had been pretty much formed. The task was to explore them.

...We were discussing whether writing is communal, whether the input of other people—for example, an editor—is useful or even necessary. I think the larger question here is the nature of reading—what it means to read a book. This affects the question of writing a book. In the past, reading a book was for the most part an isolating experience. Father Ong writes of "an individual isolated with a text." That you were communicating with the author of the book is of course true, but your situation was nonetheless an isolated one. As education began to be more widespread, that sense of isolation—a "dear reader" alone with a book—began to diminish. *At this point, I think, many people associate reading a book with taking a course*—a course with a teacher and with others participating. Reading here becomes communal. Even after the courses are ended, readers remain less isolated. They form readers' groups to discuss the books they read. These groups are to some extent versions of the classes they have taken. Again, reading is now understood to be a communal experience, something that involves both discussion and other people. I think this notion carries over into writing—especially because so many writers have taken courses in creative writing. Writing too now involves others, involves discussion. Does not feel complete unless that factor is involved. When as a child I read *Look Homeward, Angel*, I was in ecstasy. My response was to try to BE Thomas Wolfe, to write something that placed me in the same state of mind that his work had placed me in. You need of course to be liberated from that impulse, to allow a favorite writer to become an element rather than the whole, but the impulse is a primary one. The last thing I wished to do was to discuss the book with others. I wanted to *be* the book; I didn't want to be its critic. But I have to admit that there are many ways in which our culture is moving away from the notion of the lone individual—a notion which is in many ways alas the attraction of Donald Trump. Trump is almost a parody of the individual but he is functioning in a society which is clearly moving towards more communal modes.

It can of course be objected that Thomas Wolfe worked with editors. He did indeed. But I didn't know that when I read *Look Homeward, Angel*—and I would have been surprised if I had known it. *O Lost* has since been published. It's clear that one of Perkins' primary tasks was to make Wolfe's manuscript into something that looked more like a conventional novel. My own sense was astonishment that you could do what Wolfe was doing in a "novel." Please don't mistake my position here. I think the notion of the "individual" is a profoundly mistaken one and I regard all writing as collaborative. But when you are making discoveries—as I was when I wrote my choral pieces—you are more likely to be collaborating with the mighty dead rather than with the living, especially those living who have not yet made the discoveries you are making.

I felt as I wrote that I should listen only to those people who could demonstrate to me that they understood what I was TRYING to do—and it was rare to find someone like that. I'm still a bit surprised if someone likes my work, especially the more "experimental" pieces. In this situation the writer must function as his/her own internal critic, his/her own editor AS S/HE WRITES. It seems to me that the point of it all is to enter that state of mind in which poetry is possible. It is from that point of view that criticism is possible, so that both "creation" and "criticism" are happening simultaneously. This doesn't mean that you can't make an adjustment after the fit is over but it does mean that I don't believe in revision as the key to good writing. I am suggesting that the writer should open him/herself not to an editor after the piece is finished but to the chorus of people in his/her own head as the work is progressing.

*

BAMBI LAKE, COMPOSER/PERFORMER

Have you heard of Bambi Lake
I didn't till she died
Jesus "Jaded Lady" is wonderful
Jesus she was a hell of a singer
What sounds came
From that wide open mouth
How expressive were her thin arms
Jesus how can you live in a country
Where nobody has heard of Bambi Lake
How can a great artist die
As she died
And there are not thousands in the streets
Lamenting
As I lament now

Is it Trump or Biden
Or the foul history of this vicious, violent, incommodious land

At eighty, from my position of mind as multiplicity, I am continually trying to gather together all the "fragmentary evidences" I can find—trying, even in a brief poem, to bring them into some sort of "unity." I know that this is an impossible task, but I think it's worth the effort. Part of what I love about Bambi Lake was that the figure created was a walking maze of contradictions: male/female, performer/confessional (one might say professional/confessional), seducer/self-pityer. The contradictions were not resolved, only presented. Yet the figure was alive, vivid, moving before us. I understand that: a living, vivid chaos shining with life.

This perception suggests that each fragment I produce generates another and another. Nothing is complete in itself; everything is in motion, everything tends towards more. (*Revision*, I once wrote, *is addition, not subtraction*.) The result is a lot of writing, a lot of fragmentary evidences. The hope is that it is all (or at least most of it) vivid. It doesn't have to—to use Pound's notorious word— "cohere." But the pull towards coherence is also part of it. If I had never read Gertrude Stein I would never have written in certain ways. The same is true about so many others. You are constantly engaging with people who write better than you do, constantly learning, expanding. That's what it means to be a writer. "On the road."

*

WHITENESS 2020

Americans have been talking a good deal these days about "white privilege" and "white supremacy." Thirty years ago I wrote an essay called "Multiculturalism and the Media." It was delivered as a speech at the Commonwealth Club of California in 1990 and later published first in Ishmael Reed's marvelous anthology, *MultiAmerica* (Viking, 1997) and then in my book, *O Powerful Western Star* (2000). The speech was also quoted from and discussed in Walt Harrington's 1992 book, *Crossings: A White Man's Journey Into Black America.* I want to quote from it here.

According to the *Oxford English Dictionary*, the first appearance in print of the word "white" meaning "A white man; a person of a race distinguished by a light complexion," was in 1671. The second was in 1726. The speaker is a ship's captain:

> There may be about 20000 Whites (or I should say Portuguese, for they are none of the whitest,) and about treble that number of Slaves.

The term "Caucasian" is even later:

> Of or belonging to the region of the Caucasus; a name given by Blumenbach (*a* 1800) to the 'white' race of mankind, which he derived from this region.

"Through the centuries of the slave trade," writes Earl Conrad in his interesting book, *The Invention of the Negro*,

> the word race was rarely if ever used...Shakespeare's Shylock uses the words tribe, nation, but not race. The Moor in *Othello* calls himself black and the word slave is several times used, but not race. The word does not appear in the King James Version of the Bible in any context other than as running a race. The Bible refers to nations and says: "God made the world and all things therein; and hath made of one blood all nations of men for to dwell on all the face of the earth." The Bible, with all its violence and its incessant warfare between peoples, does not have racist references to tribes, groups, provinces, nations, men.

And again, on the subject of slavery:

> The traffic grew with the profits—the shuttle service importing human chattel to America in over-crowded ships.
> It was on these ships that we find the beginnings— the first crystallizations—of the curious doctrine which was to be called "white supremacy"...Among the first white men to develop attitudes of supremacy were the slaveship crews.

Hand in hand with what Mr. Conrad calls "the invention of the Negro" goes the invention of "the white man."

My young son came home from school one day and told me that he had seen some t shirts which had the equivalent of the phrase,

"Black is Beautiful" on them. (I believe the phrase was in fact "Black by Popular Demand.") He complained that he couldn't wear a shirt saying, "White is Beautiful" or "White by Popular Demand." I said, "That's true. But you *could* wear a shirt saying 'Italian is Beautiful' or 'Irish is Beautiful' or 'Spanish is Beautiful.'" The point is that *white is not an ethnic group*: it has no traditions, no culture.

But if it is not an ethnic group, what is it?

I think the answer is that white is an indication of dominance. It is always involved at some level with what Kipling called "the white man's burden." "White" in this sense is an indication of power, or of the struggle for power, or of power's lack. In the entry from the O.E.D. which I quoted a moment ago, the rhetorical opposite of "Whites" is not "Blacks" but "Slaves":

> There may be about 20000 Whites (or I should say Portuguese, for they are none of the whitest,) and about treble that Number of Slaves.

To be "white" is to engage in dominance behavior. Insofar as one does not engage in dominance behavior one is not white. But one remains Italian or Irish or German or Swedish or Jewish or whatever. *The only way for the "majority" to conceive of itself as a majority is to conceive of itself as white: without whiteness there are only "minorities."*

To speak of multiculturalism, therefore, is to speak of a way of seeing the world without whiteness—though one has to admit that whiteness (power, dominance) is much in evidence. We create it daily in our interplay with others. We create it as well by refusing to recognize the ethnicity—the genetic make-up—that we all carry with us into the world.

It was Ishmael Reed's brilliant perception that the disintegration of the notion of "the white man" brought forth the liberation of the ethnicities of which we are all a part. His organizations, The Before Columbus Foundation and PEN Oakland, are made up of various ethnic persuasions, *none of which identify as white*. That these ethnicities include the Irish, the Italians, and others that people conventionally think of as white is all the more important to stress. A long time ago, a friend of mine and I wrote a song called "There's No Man Like a White Man." I don't remember much of the song, but the ending was,

> I once built a snow man
> And put him in the hall
> With a white man
> there's no man
> at all.

Multiculturalism implies a continual effort of construction and deconstruction. It allows us to test our concepts by bringing them home, taking them inside, and seeing whether we end up with something more solid than a puddle of water. What does it mean to be Italian American? What does it mean to be Irish American? Did Columbus discover America or did he invade it? What does it mean to be white?

> I once built a snow man
> And put him in the hall
> With a white man
>   there's no man
>   at all.

How do we get rid of this bump on the log, this pothole in the road, the white man? We can begin by noting that it never really existed.

*

In an email Heather Cox Richardson asked her readers about American themes and an American narrative. I answered:

There are hundreds of themes in American history, some big, some small. One of the most problematical has to do with the definition of "freedom." "Freedom"—so often invoked—is one of the most problematical terms in the American language. In some contexts it means essentially capitalism; in others, it means, precisely, getting rid of capitalism. The word is shot through as well with resonances from our revolutionary past—a past that in many ways has no influence on our present except as a rhetorical device. The great American gesture of becoming an adult, especially for men but for both men and women, is to find some means of removing yourself from the family, to become an autonomous entity, an "individual" (by etymology "undivided"). This is echoed in the old notion that when your neighbor's smoke gets a little too close, it's time to move West. This idea arises ultimately from Plato's myth of the cave in "The Republic" and it gets itself Christianized in various ways: in this concept, freedom is essentially removing yourself from the womb. This removal is of course often represented as a struggle because the womb always has a considerable hold on you. Current Trump supporters seem to understand freedom in this way. But there is another notion of freedom: Hannah Arendt expounds it quite well in *The Human Condition*. In Plato, the soul is in effect re-born: it removes itself from the theater in which it sees only false shadows (the dark womb) and enters the blinding sunlight of actuality. For Hannah Arendt, on the other hand, freedom involves finding the right kind of theater, the right kind of womb: for her, freedom involves recognizing the place and desires of others. Freedom is not possible unless this condition is met. We do not remove ourselves from others but deliberately interact with them in order to realize our own individuality. Freedom here is a social concept rather than a gesture towards individual isolation. I think the United States is moving towards this notion of freedom, but it is doing so in a confused and often dispiriting way. Still, these two notions of freedom are at the center of so many of our debates. A new American narrative should recognize them and bring them into consciousness. As it is, each is simply and separately assumed to be true—"the way things are."

Another great theme that should be mentioned is perhaps at the heart of all the other themes: the theme of "equality." When Jefferson wrote that "all men are created equal," even he did not fully believe that statement. Yet he made it, and his words have resonated throughout American history. Walt Whitman also took equality to be the central fact about America. His poem, "America," begins, "Centre of equal daughters, equal sons, / All, all alike endear'd." (Note that he included women, not just men.) Whitman too did not fully believe what he said—or at least did not believe it all of the time. Indeed, never has equality in this sense been fully realized, but the notion is repeated again and again. The problem is that "equality" is an ideal trying to be a fact but remaining in many respects an ideal. We can "believe" in an ideal but nonetheless not find it to be something affecting our everyday lives. We can believe in Jesus, for example, and, without sensing the contradiction or even being genuinely hypocritical, do things that Jesus would never approve of. That is the case with equality. Once it moves from the realm of ideal into the realm of fact, it becomes immediately problematical. This split between equality as an ideal and equality as a fact is one of the great aspects of American history and what we might call the American Mind, and it is certainly being fought over right now, in the streets as well as in individual consciousness. An insistence that ideals must be activated—made real—and the revelation of the historical tension between ideal and fact might also be part of a new American narrative.

The notion that history *is* a narrative—not "facts," a story—should also be included. We are tale-tellers and we will of course wish to hew as much as possible to actuality but a tale is a tale. Democracy is fundamentally a story.

*

DONALD AT THE BAT

The Trumpville slugger is up at bat. The bases are loaded. Bottom of the ninth. Two out.
Covid-19 sends a fast one across the plate.
STEEEEEERIKE ONE says the Umpire.
The slugger grits his teeth. He taps the bat on the plate.
Covid-19 throws a high curve ball across the plate.
STEEEEEERIKE TWO says the Umpire.
Strike? says the slugger. What are you, a Democrat? You must be a Democrat.
STEEEEEERIKE TWO says the Umpire.
Grrrrrrr, tweets the slugger. Anger is fueling him now. He knows this game. This is HIS game. He will not let another pitch go by. Grrrrr.
Covid-19 winds up. Sends out another fast one, this one with a hop.
The slugger SWINGS with a force like a hurricane. Whoosh goes the bat as it whirls on its path.

What could resist a blow like that?
STEEEEEERIKE THREE says the Umpire. The slugger has
missed the ball!
Oh, somewhere politicians
Are wooing willing crowds
Somewhere the sun is shining
And the sky is free of clouds
Somewhere the stores are open
And consumers move about
But there is no joy in Trumpville:
Mighty Donald has struck out.

...

TRIOLET

The bells are ringing all over Paris
To declare the end of a despicable reign
Four years this man continued to harass
Us—the bells are ringing all over Paris
At long long last he will not embarrass
Good folk from the Potomac to the Seine
The bells are ringing all over Paris
To declare the end of a deadly reign.

*

BRECHT

Is *Aufstieg und Fall der Stadt Mahagonny* (*Rise and Fall of the City of Mahagonny*) about "helplessness"? The concluding chorus is brutally insistent: *Cannot help a dead man.* In the play within a play, Brecht has brought the supreme example of authority onto his stage: God. And he has shown people saying No to God. *If the people of Mahagonny can say No to God, can't we say No to a play?* Can't we respond to "Cannot help ourselves and you and no one" by saying "No! That's not true: we *can* help the living"? It's an extraordinary moment because the supposedly didactic Brecht is being anything but explicit here. (In a 1926 "Conversation" he insists that "I leave the maximum freedom of interpretation. The sense of my plays is immanent. You have to fish it out for yourself.") In *Mahagonny* Brecht is taking the chance that his audience (even a highly sophisticated member of the audience like Martin Esslin) will completely misunderstand him. On the other hand, those who get the point will (like me) remember it forever: I heard *Mahagonny* at the age of twenty, and I am still talking about it! Though the playwright has of course deliberately prompted the response in the audience, *the response has occurred in the audience's consciousness*, not in the play itself. The play is in this sense dialectical. Brecht is challenging his audience to *disagree with his play. He is not only trying to "instruct" the audience; he is trying to transform it.* This it seems to me is political poetry at its finest, addressed as much to the people who disagree with you as to the people who agree with you. It is an ultimately benevolent *attack* upon the audience, not preaching to the choir. In "Theatre

for Learning" Brecht remarks that "The audience in the epic
theatre says":

> I wouldn't have thought that.—People
> shouldn't do things like that.—That's
> extremely odd, almost unbelievable.—
> This has to stop.—This person's suffering
> shocks me, because there might be a way
> out for him.—This is great art: nothing in
> it is self-evident.—I laugh over the
> weeping, I weep over the laughing.

And he adds,

> Oil, inflation, war, social struggles, the family,
> religion, wheat, the meat-packing industry,
> [become] subjects for theatrical portrayal.

…

Look at those birds: lovers
circling
you came from Havana
years ago
I came from Alaska
I, Jimmy—
Seven years in the cold
in the snow-covered woods
I made it
and spent it—
now there's nothing left of me

…

WE DON'T NEED
HURRICANES

WE DON'T NEED
TYPHOONS
WE CAN DO
WHATEVER THEY DO
BETTER—

...

don't let them fool you
    it's the business
you don't come back
    of the future
day's in the doorway
    to be
but you feel
    dangerous
the night wind

...

there's nothing but life
    I first heard it over fifty years ago
you stand with the beasts
    "ein mensch ist kein tier"
they'll use you if you let them
    At eighty, I hear it again,
        Lenya's growly, inimitable voice

    the night wind moves me to tears

*

FROM *YEARS POEM*: WHAT HAVE THE YEARS TAKEN AWAY?

Adelle, Adelle foremost, Adelle and again, Adelle
Hoppinjohn, meat sauce, beignets, fruit cakes
Foods that bring tears
Because she made them
Her haiku, written on anything
Scraps of newspaper, anything
Her conversation
Strands of my hair that used to flower
The ease of walking (the gift of sciatica)
My old tap shoes
Thinness
Ability to fit into certain clothes
Ability to wash dishes or brush teeth without tiring
Ability to get through a day without a nap
Ability to read a boring book without falling asleep
Friendship, even love, of certain people .
And now, watching it, John Fitzgerald Kennedy's
Eulogy
For Robert Frost
(Written by Arthur Schlesinger, Jr.,
Edited heavily by Kennedy)
Brings tears.
John Fitzgerald Kennedy's
Eulogy
For Robert Frost
Displays clearly
All *we* have lost
Robert Frost brought an unsparing instinct for reality
To bear on the platitudes and pieties of society
Kennedy's Eulogy
Is Praise
Of the poetic impulse
(Which, for him, is not separate from the political impulse)
It tears

At the heart of our lost nation
Frost saw poetry as the means of saving power from itself
What dark truths do we live among now
Since these men died?
What city
Shines now
Upon what hill?

*

ELI, ELI

"It would be bad enough if I were the next-door neighbor.
But this is like God doing it. Jesus doing it."
                    —"First Person: The Confession of Father X"

Father O'Fondle comes to town
Hoping that your pants are down
What's your sport, me lad, says he
Can you sit upon me knee
(I have sport enow for thee!)
Let me look upon your dangle
Try Confession from THIS angle
What I beat is not a drum
Who put the "cum" in "Vobiscum"?
(Which of you dare call me "scum"?)
Bishop, Bishop, though I'm lacking
I know you will send me packing
To another parish bright
Where I'm sure I'll do all right
I'll bring "God" to them and theirs
And they'll remember in their prayers
In the night when dreams are wet
They will see me smiling yet

Holding out God's helping hand—
There's a sweet and sacred band!
Till Hell turns to ice and freezes
You'll make Love to me—and Jesus
I'll apply the priestly arts
To your troubled private parts
Here, my lad, 's a welcome solace
Let me touch your throbbing phallus
Hear the Sacred Choir thrumming
As I prepare my Second Coming!
Father O'Fondle, troubled man
Needing love, and under ban
In such desire for the Son,
Would I have done as you have done?

*

GP SKRATZ / *SUNDAE MISSILE: THE MASS OF THE CHURCH OF THE CENTER THAT WILL NOT HOLD*

I first came upon GP Skratz's *Sundae Missile: The Mass of the Church of the Center That Will Not Hold* when he performed it, with the aid of his stepson, the late Tim Lemon, on December 20, 1987 at my poetry series at Larry Blake's Restaurant in Berkeley, California. Skratz was wearing faux priest's attire as he intoned,

ANOMALY POT ROAST, EDSEL SEA,
EXPERIENCE SANK DEEP. ALMOND.

Sundae Missile is a "homophonic" translation into English of "the pre-Vatican Council Latin version" of the Roman Catholic Mass— something which both Skratz and I had experienced in childhood and had rejected as we grew older. To say that something is a "homophonic" translation is to say that it attempts to translate the *sounds*—not necessarily the meanings—of a foreign text into English. The most famous homophonic translation was executed by Celia and Louis Zukofsky, whose 1969 *Catullus* (Cape Goliard Press) is a "sounded" version of the entirety of the Pagan poet's work. Here is a sample of the original Latin of the Mass along with Skratz's "translation." This is The Sanctus in English, Latin and Skratz.

THE SANCTUS

Holy, Holy, Holy,
Lord God of Hosts
Heaven and earth
Are full of Thy Glory
Hosanna in the highest
Blessed is he who comes in the name of the Lord
Hosanna in the highest

Sanctus, Sanctus, Sanctus,
Dominus Deus Sabaoth.
Pleni sunt caeli et terra
Gloria tua.
Hosanna in excelsis.
Benedictus qui venit in nomine Domini.
Hosanna in excelsis.

sandwich, sandwich, sandwich,
dynamite days of savagery.
plenty of quality error
storybook toes.

o zany sin asbestos.
banner pick-ax key bandit anonymous domino.
o zany sin asbestos.

Sundae Missile is clearly reminiscent not only of James Joyce but
of Gertrude Stein's *Tender Buttons*. But there is something else as
well. For those who can hear it, the sound of the Latin is *there* just
as surely as it is in the verse of Milton's *Paradise Lost. Yet it is
also absent.* There is not a word of Latin in Skratz's text, though
Latin informs absolutely everything the author has produced. The
status of Latin here is not unlike the status of Jesus in the Mass
itself—and, beyond that, in the lives of those who have lived
through (and beyond) Catholicism. *Jesus is now an absent
presence in the world, just as Latin is an absent presence in this
text. Sundae Missile* is great fun—and proposes "merriment" in
place of the solemn "verily"—but it is also a genuinely religious
document. It is not only "The Mass of the Church of the Center
That Will Not Hold" but the Mass of the liberation of the psyche
from the hold of hundreds of years of teaching and prejudice and
superstition and ecstasy and brilliance of thought; from a system
whose slow crumbling can be felt by only a few well-tuned
seismographs but which nevertheless—despite the "popularity" of
the current Pope—seems to be genuinely, historically on the way
out:

sickness egg nog demented mouse terror bus nozzle.

>egg nog in darkness in tents of the omen.
>subliminal news tomorrow.
>almond.

And yet, and yet. Seeing the production at Larry Blake's, my friend Larry Eigner remarked, "Blasphemy was in the air." But despite the parodies, the strange language, the challenges, the Mass—the genuine article—easily survives all this folderol. Parody is a mixed form. In a way it is an attack upon its object, but in another sense parody presents the deep longing for the thing itself, the desire for it to be present in a way that it is not. Something like that may be happening in the psyche of GP Skratz: parody as the door to Salvation. Parody insists on the presence—somewhere, if not quite here—of the very thing it seems to be attempting to demolish. "I don't care what you say about me," said George M. Cohan, "as long as you spell my name right." Benedictus qui venit in nomine Domini. Blessed is he who comes in the name of the Lord. Here is GP Skratz.

*

VISIONS & AFFILIATIONS: 1300 PAGES OF LOCALISM

In this history of "the growth of a poet's mind," I should mention my 1300-page, two-volume "chronoencyclopedia," *Visions and Affiliations: California Poetry from 1940 to 2005.*

Published by Iván Argüelles' Pantograph Press in 2011, the book generated a book about itself, *Jack Foley's Unmanageable Masterpiece* (2018) by Dana Gioia and Peter Whitfield. Gioia and Whitfield write: "In 2011 a tiny press in Berkeley published *Visions and Affiliations*, an eccentric 1300-page chronology of post-war California literature in two massive paperbound folio volumes. With no commercial distribution or publicity, the book sold about two hundred copies and soon vanished from sight—but not from the memory of the small audience that read it. Some of them considered the elaborate time line the first adequate account of California's complex and contradictory literary life. Others recognized Foley's radical innovation in changing how literary history could be written. A few even considered the strange, sprawling, yet compulsively readable tomes an oddball masterpiece."

This is from my contribution to the book:

The problem with doing a book like *Visions and Affiliations* is that you're always digging up new things which sometimes contradict what you thought you "had." Nothing is "secure." If you let yourself be too aware of the utter endlessness of the project, you're lost—you'll stop doing it—so you keep saying, "Ok, that's fine, it's finished now." But of course there are many instances in which what seems to be "finished" turns out to be merely the beginning of something. You *know* the project is endless—and constantly getting away from you—but you do what you can to forget that fact. And you comfort yourself with the momentary, perhaps illusory insights that arise as you go through. Slippery history!

When songwriter/performer Marshall Barer blandly asked a young woman in his audience, "What's your sign, dear?" she answered, "Slippery when wet!" Trying to write history is dealing with wet. That's why historians so often rely on the work of "colleagues." The work of others offers some foundation. But colleagues too are often nothing but apple carts waiting to be upset.

I think that all this activity reflects that self-questioning which lies at the heart of Heidegger's *"Dasein"*—a being which places its own being in question. It's not that there is no "ground," but that any "ground" you find is tentative, temporary, temporal. For many years, God was the *Urgrund*, the ground of grounds. But once God goes—and God is gone—innumerable grounds appear, each with its bit of truth and untruth. From James Harkness's introduction to Michel Foucault's *This is not a Pipe*:

"Things are cast adrift, more or less like one another without any of them being able to claim the privileged status of 'model' for all the rest. Hierarchy gives way."

If there is any *Urgrund* in this book, it is the constantly changing, endlessly conflictive fabric of time.

...

Someone said he thought that *Visions and Affiliations* was a fine "reference book." I told him that I didn't think it was a reference book at all. If it were really a reference work, it would have to have a better index—or be laid out in such a way that you could find people easily. It's more an epic, a simulation of world in motion: I say at the conclusion that the book's *"Urgrund"* is "the constantly changing, endlessly conflictive fabric of time."

Wikipedia: Kevin Owen Starr "was an American historian and California's State Librarian, best known for his multi-volume series on the history of California, collectively called 'Americans and the California Dream.'" I didn't know Kevin Starr, but a friend suggested that I send my book to him. This is Kevin Starr's ecstatic response to *Visions and Affiliations*, left on my phone machine and here transcribed: "I'm just sitting here overwhelmed overwhelmed by the achievement of the two volume *Visions and Affiliations*...absolutely overwhelmed by it—absolutely overwhelmed...This is an extraordinary piece of work...extraordinary...there should be a *major major* review of this...but before that happens I want to talk to you...please phone me...congratulations...what an achievement...what an achievement."

Others have responded in that ecstatic way. I think what is happening is this: Most—pretty much all—books have an authorial presence, of which we are aware: we know that there is *someone* speaking to us, making commentaries, organizing things. In this book, the authorial presence is minimized, almost not there. "Jack Foley" says things, but he is one character among many characters who say things. Instead, there are many, many entries, many "voices," many relating to one another, sometimes echoing one another—but there is no single "person" obviously organizing all that. The reader is left far more on his/her own. There are many, many patterns to be found.

I quote Michel Foucault in "A Note on This Book": "I mean the disorder in which a large number of possible orders glitter separately." I think that's a pretty good description of *Visions and Affiliations*. There is no *one* order which covers everything, tells you what everything means, but there are many, many "possible orders" manifesting throughout. A reader like Starr notices these patterns and, lacking an authorial presence, begins to put them together *for him/herself.* What he/she "discovers" is his/her own capacity for ordering material—which is to say *his/her mind.* I think it's this discovery that brought Starr to his sense of ecstasy; he is crediting me, but it is his own mind that is "overwhelming." He told me that he sensed "the flow of life" (the phrase is from C.P. Snow) throughout my book.

At any rate, that's why I put this as the very last thing:

It's one of the convictions of our "democratic," "free market" society that you can sell *anything* if you present it in the right way. So people think they don't care for poetry-product. So let's present it more like rock n roll product. Then people will like it. Let's add music to it. Or show people how much "fun" it is, how it allows them to be more individualistic, to "express themselves." Then people will like it. Or show them that it doesn't have to be obscure and difficult, "intellectual." See, it's accessible, *this* poetry isn't difficult. Then they'll like it. What of Rilke's statement: *"Du mußt dein Leben ändern"* / "You must change your life" ("Archaic Torso of Apollo")? Here the notion is not to change the "product" in some way but to *change the people perceiving the product*. The notion is still transformative, but it is transformative in a different sense. A student remarked to Martin Heidegger, "I like philosophy but what can you *do* with philosophy?" Heidegger replied that the student was asking the wrong question. The real question was not, "What can you do with philosophy?" The real question was, "What will philosophy"—read, poetry—"do with you?"

*

**VIDEO STATEMENT FOR *LITTERATEUR RW /*
DEFINITION OF POETRY**
http://www.litterateurrw.com/

If democracy means rule by the people, then the Electoral College is an affront to democracy. I'm Jack Foley. Today is Election Day, November 3rd, 2020. I want to talk to you about art. The Electoral College is a way of avoiding the will of the people; art is a way for the people's voice to make itself heard. Never before have we so needed political consciousness. Never before have we so needed art.

I would like to promote a new online/print magazine with a French name and initials that mean something in English. *Litterateur RW*: *Litterateur Redefining World.* It does not come from New York or San Francisco or London or Dublin or Paris or Berlin or New South Wales. It comes from Kerala, India. It is global in its intent and vehemently hip—woke—in its procedures. You will often find accents here and syntactical constructions that are not what is usually referred to as "standard" English. Long years ago, James Joyce understood that the voice of the people did not express itself in standard English. His *Finnegans Wake*—though in English—is also an attack upon the English language, which for Joyce was simultaneously his own language and the language of the oppressor. Americans understand this contradiction all too well. These words of mine will appear in the current issue of *Litterateur RW*:

I was asked for my definition of poetry. I wrote this: Despite popular usage, the opposite of prose is not poetry: the opposite of prose is verse. Prose is a *form*, just as the sonnet or the villanelle is a form. What we call "poetry" can occur as an element of any form, verse or prose. Poetry is an intensification of words so that they leap beyond their immediate meaning and evoke contexts that arise purely from imagination. What makes a poem a poem is its accomplishment of this event. Verbal "music"—not quite the same as the "music" produced by an instrument or a singing voice—is an aspect as well so we may say that poetry is a musical, linguistic evocation of otherness, of something beyond the words in their initial and immediate appearance.

To put it another way, poetry can be hope. You will find plenty of that in *Litterateur RW*.

I wrote this as a form of poetry and a form of hope:

NOVEMBER 3, 2020 (ELECTION DAY): FATHER TO SON

I spoke to my son of the rebirth
of progressive political thought. I spoke to my son
of possibility. I spoke to him
of the hope for a more just, more loving
world, of a new birth of the best aspects
of the 1960s—so easily parodied or denied.
I spoke to my son of a world
my generation failed to give him
and which I would have wished for him
and his loving wife. I do not know
what today will bring, perhaps a failure
of our hopes, but hope is
the sweet air in our lungs.
I spoke to my son of the need for love

*

If

we cast our historical net wide enough, we begin to believe that poetry has been usurped by prose. But it is possible to reverse the usurpation: to write something that seems almost to be prose until—until it has been transformed and has acquired, despite its prosaic elements, the power of a poem. Free verse is the laboratory in which this alchemy now usually takes place—William Carlos Williams was a great master—but it is of course also possible for the transformation to occur in the realm of traditional verse. Robert Frost or George Szirtes. "Poetry" is not a form but the accomplishment of linguistic transformation, not a form but an event. It is a place in which intuition and knowledge dance together. *The "magic" the poet performs is real, but it is nothing other than the creation of "poetry."*

*

WHAT ABOUT ALL THIS WRITING?

kaleidoscopic
mind
looks for itself
in every tear and purchase
seeks to know

in every random
rock & centipede / every fairy tale
frog / tree limb / ballerina / fire / butcher's block

itself

•

kaleidoscopic
strange
mind
the notion
looks for itself
that
in every tear and purchase
mind
seeks to know
is separate
in every random
from
rock & centipede / every fairy tale
body's
frog / tree limb / ballerina / fire / butcher's block
hulk

itself

•

"What about all this writing?" William Carlos Williams asked in 1923. The constant quasi-erotic need for movement, for the creation of the "new." I am in this a true child of Modernism. The creators of the *polis,* Heidegger remarks in *An Introduction to Metaphysics,* are themselves *apolis:* hence arises their need to create. When I entered poetry I was under the deep influence of the voices that had flooded over me in old radio. I felt that both writing and the performance of writing were slighting the "oral tradition." My work—especially my choral work—was a response to that. Later, I began to think of writing as a search for "selfhood," except that I found myself denying the existence of the "individual self" in favor of the notion of "multiplicity" and asserting as a kind of mantra that "some parts of the mind don't know what other parts of the mind are doing." How was it possible to express that situation in a poem? I began to think as well that the very search for one's "identity" issued in a fiction—that the very act of self (one cannot get away from the word) contemplation was in some way delusional. There may be a moment of what some philosophers would call "authenticity," but it exists only in the deepest moment of a poem or a work of art and vanishes immediately afterwards, though we remember its presence and seek it out again.

Mind moves and it is possible that the movement itself is as close as we can come to a perception of reality. At our most authentic, at our realist, we are not entities but movement, movement involving all the things that have come crowding into our welcoming consciousness throughout our life, like the ghosts in the eleventh book of *The Odyssey*. The notion that we are "individuals" (undivided entities) is as false as the rain predicted on a sunny day. Life is a journey, but it is a journey in all directions at once as the universe or the life force or whatever you wish to call it (kaleidoscopic mind) makes use of us to see what it has been doing for all these years—or to adjust, to make changes, to see "what will suffice."

*

HOMAGE TO HILLARY LEFTWICH: HOW SAD IT WAS WHEN THE SKY

We drove past the circus tent on the way to the mortuary. A freak standing there waved at us. When he smiled he showed his gold tooth. I said, "Mama, when will we get there?" She said, "Shhhhh, child, it isn't far." I said, "Mama, why won't you tell me who's dead?" She said, "You'll see when we get there." The sky was a strange pink that day. I thought it looked like apocalypse. "You'll know apocalypse when you see it," said Papa. "Only open your heart to Jesus." On the far ridge of that mountain there lived a murderer. We knew but the police didn't. He was a nice, gentle man and we didn't want the police to find him. I heard he had killed five people but they weren't friends of mine either. There are people I wouldn't mind seeing dead. Maybe the president. Mama says I shouldn't feel that way. Mama says every human soul is unique and every soul has its reasons, even a murderer's soul. I told her I didn't believe in the soul and she slapped my face. The mortuary loomed up ahead of us. It was smaller than I thought it might be but it didn't look that different from a regular building.

We went inside and were met by a man in a black suit. He had thin, slicked back hair. He looked southern, like us. "You'll want to see the body," he said and led us into a small room that smelled like stale paint. There was a small coffin there, like the coffin of a child. Its lid was open. When I peered inside I wasn't surprised to see my body there. I was dressed in my best suit and my hair was combed back in an unnatural way. "You see," said Mama. "It's very important to have a soul. Folks who don't believe in souls grow up to be the freaks in the circus." I thought how sad it was when the sky seemed to tell you the days of the earth were numbered and soon we would all be goners.

*

SHE WHO EMPTIES ME OF ALL BUT NIGHT: IN IMITATION OF GHAREEB ISKANDER

To find language
Adequate
To

Ash is everywhere now
Like snow

Your eyes
Still search me.
In the false dawn I awake

It is all
But

Impossible

Reaching for the fork
I accidentally find
knife

Not looking not longing not

In the dream of the wild plain
The grasses point
Toward the redeeming line

You are
Our Lady of the Flowers
Thief's Journal
Miracle of the Rose

...

"I was close to biting one of your tender fingers
that night
when the sky poured its wrath upon us"

It was neither day
nor the semblance of
neither dawn

nor dusk

neither the foul embrace
of the serpent
nor the sweet taste of the rose
You are the Book of Sand
the Book of Night
the crepuscular figure

I see as I die

...

Beloved, beloved, beloved

she whose arms encircle me

she whose tender

wings embrace my sleeping eyes

she who returns

after days on the sea

she whose voice

is like the silence

of the unending

spaces

between the stars

...

she who empties me

of all

but night

*

THE SEARCH FOR A LANGUAGE

Recently I have begun to think of Modernism as the search for a language—a language in which it would be possible to express that Modernist word, the "new," what Hart Crane called a "transition from a decayed culture toward a reorganization of human evaluations." I would include movements such as Dada and Futurism, texts such as Pound's *Cantos*, Eliot's *Waste Land*, Vallejo's *Trilce*, Joyce's attacks on the English language in *Finnegans Wake*, Stein's *Tender Buttons*, Yeats' attempt to create a sacred, "occult" language of poetry in *The Wind Among the Reeds*, Hart Crane's work, influenced by Ouspensky, Heidegger's restructuring of German in *Sein und Zeit*, Mayakovsky, Artaud's wild cries in his "radiodiffusion," *Pour En Finir Avec Le Jugement De Dieu*, Wittgenstein's speculations, Zukofsky's homophonic translations of Catullus, many others. More recent work might be included as well: Iván Argüelles' wild, erudite, simultaneously Surrealist, Classical, and South Asian mentations, Jake Berry's *Brambu Drezi*, John M. Bennett's visual-literary work, excursions into the asemic, again many others. Some of my own wilder pieces, such as this attempt in *scriptio continua*, come out of this desire as well, I think:

MARVELOUSUNREALITYFICTIONSSTORIESPOETRYHAVI
NGNOCONNECTION TO SOIDISANT"REALITY"PURE
IMAGINATIONFLIGHTSOF FANCYFANCYFLIGHTS
THEWORD"BONFIRE"

ACORKANDBOTTLEABUSHELANDAPECKERPROBABLEC
AUSELIGHTFINGERSONTHELISSOMEHEAVENLYHEAVIE
SMILITANTMARGINIMAGINEDPÓGA(IRISHFORKISSES)

LOWERLIPSOFDESIREBREEZEWINGSWINGOFTHENIGHT
FREEDOMTHESEA

FASHIONSANDCELEBRITYRESHAPETHEFUTURESIGNTH
EPETITIONLETUSREMEMBERTHENATIONALSYSTEMLET
USREMEMBERAMERICAMEDESVINCULODELMARIAMFR
EEDFROMTHEBURDENOFTHESEA

WARMPASTELSHANDSINTHELIGHTSUNSPLENDORINSO
MECITYYOUNGSTILLSTILLYOUNGSOFTHAIRSPILLING

WATERMOVINGLEAVESFALLINGAUTUMNEYESTRAVELI
NGSKYSHIPLIGHTSMOKEBEAUTY   .

FIERCER THAN THE SUN:
THE ACTIONS OF MEN

Note: *me desvinculo del mar*—a line from César Vallejo
(translated here as "I am freed from the burden of the sea")

My friend Iván Argüelles answered this piece with:

FABULOUSLYUNTOLDMIRACULOUSLYREFOLDEDSHIPS
HAPEDENTERPRISEOFWORDSUNBOUNDUNLEASHEDSW
ARMING
THEPAGEUNWRITTENFREEDOMLESSTHANLIGHTTHESU
NAMANIFOLDEXPERIENCEOFBREATHATONCEAND
NOMORE

This language is not achieved but continually attempted, continually indicated as possible. I recently thought of the attempt to achieve it as the sounds coming from the severed head of Orpheus:

ORPHÉE

"Do you speak French?"
—*Suzanne Verdal*

c'est la tête qui chante
après la mort
après la grande Perte
c'était le projet

du Modernisme
de chercher une langue
nouvelle

une langue

qui chante
après la mort

une langue
sans histoire
comme la langue
des oiseaux

je suis le poète
de cette langue

impossible

la tête d'orphée
qui chante avec une force très grande

comme un aveugle
qui tape à la machine

*

Time may be a river, but it is a river that continually turns back upon itself, a river that brings its body of burdens back to the deep sea.

*

FINALE: AT THE TOMB OF JACK FOLEY

I know what becomes of the piggy
If the piggy's unable to scram

It's the piggy's sad fate
To be served on a plate
And be known by the cognomen, "ham."

Miraculously preserved by the miracle of microfiche
His poems influence only those who have not read them.
Here he lies
Which is not to say that he didn't lie in other places too.
Language came to him when he was fifteen
And told him, "I am about to offer you a career
Which will give you neither money nor power nor influence
Nor any special capacity with the fairer sex.
Mostly you'll be ignored. How about it?"
"Why not?" he said. "So what if I starve?" And so it began,
As it happened, starve he did not. He wrote volumes and volumes
And proclaimed his Folly to a world which,
Though bored with its distractions, yawned (or made a violent
gagging sound)
At the mere mention of the word "poetry."
Mourn for him not, dear reader, he did what he wished
Speaking his mind at every opportunity
Whether it was appropriate or not
And not minding the raspberries or raised middle fingers.
Remember what a friend said upon introducing him:
"Don't let Jack scare you." *Ars longa, Jack brevis*, Foley sighed.
His pockets—empty, but his verse was free.

*

From *Finnegans Wake*:

Then Nuvoletta reflected for the last time in her little long life and she made up all her myriads of drifting minds in one. She cancelled all her engauzements. She climbed over the bannistars; she gave a childy cloudy cry: *Nuée! Nuée!* A lightdress fluttered. She was gone. And into the river that had been a stream (for a thousand tears had gone eon her and come on her and she was stout and struck on dancing and her muddied name was Missisliffi) there fell a tear, a singult tear, the loveliest of all tears (I mean for those crylove fables fans who are 'keen' on the prettypretty commonface sort of thing you meet by hopeharrods) for it was a leaptear. But the river tripped on her by and by, lapping as though her heart was brook: *Why, why, why! Weh, O weh! I'se so silly to be flowing but I no canna stay!*

*

DECEMBER 2020

the holy season
but what is holy,
numinous
in this or any—

what can we say
opens the heart
to the larger life

I saw it as a child
in thomas gray

and thomas wolfe
and shelley
"if winter comes"

my age is my winter

the life
which james joyce identified
with a woman's disordered
thoughts
as she falls asleep

and then with the vast sea

Michael McClure on Jack Foley (2012):

BEGINNING WITH LINES BY THE POET

for JACK FOLEY

"THIS MAN LOOKS OUT AT ME
eyes full of interest and perhaps suffering
whatever he looks at registered on his face…"
Just that much and not more would be enough,
always though he is dancing like his dad, shuffling
canny strange steps of thirties and 3000 a.d.
KNOWLEDGE OF POETRY
Finds him and Adelle
opening Clyfford Still's mystery:
Let figure and ground fuse into one.
Eyes tell a little more than the ear hears.
Yes, his poetry breathes intelligence

BUT
it's also aloft with intuition.
He recreated the Batman Gallery
but did not ever touch his winged
feet on those Fillmore Street boards.
Bards welcomed him there and then,
and inspired artists painted his
IMAGINATION.
He goes on to triumph through the modes:
from archetypal Olsonian projectivity
of post-heroic deconstruction
to eructation of naughty nursery rhymes
without a solecism in sight.

Like Cocteau, "Radio Daddy"
made tubes and circuits sing Poetry
in voices of Whitman and Gertrude Stein

(and, almost, Emily Dickinson).

He
oped
airways
multiculturally,
and with catholicity
speaks the finest and sees
the highest possible
in other.
IN CREATING THE INEFFABLE
POETRY TIME LINE OF CALIFORNIA
he presented it as most effable,
and in the loop and trajectory
of the unknown, but now known,
history of the work he became
at one with
the work. (The *POEIN)*

—Did Goethe create Faust
or vice versa?—

Loving all poesy from L=A=N=G=U=A=G=E
to dangling American foot
he uncovered the root
of unpremeditated wit
AND IN THE PASTURES
flowered by their strophes,
he sings forth with his better
half,
THE LADY
A
D
E
L
L
E

:

Shepherd and shepherdess of vocable
and volta
with joyful tongue
and breeze-stroked lyra.

"Thus are things decreed by fate.
Esti gar eimarmena pantos…"

Manannan mac Lir
(Michael McClure)

Jack Foley on Michael McClure (2020):

THE KING, THE PRINCE, THE POET
for Michael McClure (October 20, 1932-May 4,
2020)

The prince is dead.
Defender of whales.
It didn't seem possible.
The great one
Who read his work at
The most famous of all
San Francisco readings
Six Gallery, 1955.
The one who voiced his poems
To the marvelous melodies

Of Ray Manzarek,
From whom Janis Joplin
Stole a song,
The one who told me,
"People who wear black
Are in mourning for themselves."
The king is dead.
The one who survived
Everything
And lived to sing of it,
The one who spoke
Chaucer in the original
So that people might know
Where our language came from.
The king, the prince, the poet
Who rose from Wichita
And embodied San Francisco
Who called to the birds near his home
Who answered.
"We were making," he told me,
"The myth of ourselves."
He survived so much
It seemed likely
That Death would make an exception
In his case
(No, he did not have Coronavirus!)
But this wonderful man
Is gone from us.
His Angel weeps.
Her name is Amy
And she will forever be
His love, his partner
Though there was another
Who loved him too.
Dear Angel, whose wings
Will have to fly in a different way
To find him now.

I loved them both
And learned from them.
She survives to build a world
Around herself in which
Michael forever is
And isn't
While she goes on.
May she fly, as she always has,
With sweet, compassionate dignity.
May her delicate hands
Build figures (embodiments) that live forever
As Michael's words
Will live forever.
There is a world
That does not die.
The Muses
Weep.

.

ELEGY

The animals are clamoring
The deer
The hawks circling
The squirrels
All the inhabitants of the zoo
The lions in the San Francisco Zoo
They are all making noises
The monkeys howl
Dogs and cats in the streets
The incredible coyotes
Strolling in the city
The fish
The whales
Even the tiny things, the ants, the bugs, mosquitos
Everything

Even the living trees
That bend to the wind
Near the water
The ocean the sand
The monkeys
They are all muttering or crying
Or howling outright
And the animals that are people
The "mammal nation"—
All these creatures know
They clamor they "complain" (in the old sense)
That the poet McClure is gone
Though they cannot
            tell you where

JACK FOLEY ON THE INTERNET

<u>Audio</u>

JACK & ADELLE FOLEY: PERFORMANCES

"Words & Books, Poetry & Writing"; "Chorus: SON(G)"; "The Current State of Poetry"; "Overture: Chorus"

Texts available in Jack Foley, *O Powerful Western Star* and Jack Foley, *Eyes* (Selected Poems)

https://soundcloud.com/john-w-foley/from-o-powerful-western-star-overture-chorus

JACK FOLEY & SANGYE LAND, *DATE: DINNER & A MOVIE 2020*

https://soundcloud.com/john-w-foley/dinner-and-a-movie-mp3?fbclid=IwAR2lW3tNW—VaVlF67baY6MEdnS1NJGLsf17Py6lPMTYdbw7ztf1M_5i9RA

<u>Video</u>

JACK AND ADELLE FOLEY: MARY RUDGE'S STAR ROVER TV (1990)

The program is in 5 parts:

1. https://www.youtube.com/watch?v=E-QgiWz8rs8&feature=related
    (Irish speech begins at 2:15)
2. https://www.youtube.com/watch?v=GexgUeDwL8c
3. https://www.youtube.com/watch?v=fzZQj2nXVrk
4. https://www.youtube.com/watch?v=hSqgqPXrQ9Y
5. https://www.youtube.com/watch?v=5GMpMPcxm_w
    (tap dance poem included in this segment: 2:36)

JACK FOLEY DAY / JUNE 5, 2010 CELEBRATION

Event Documents page that documents the public celebration of Jack Foley's life and work on June 5, 2010 with photos, official proclamation, speech, and videos:

http://eventdocuments.blogspot.com

Jack & Adelle performing:

https://www.youtube.com/watch?v=xEpvE2OgQGI&t=340s

JACK & ADELLE FOLEY ANIMATED BY BEAU BLUE

"Ballad of the Beatles"

https://www.youtube.com/watch?v=yo8eC806wmY

There are many other videos available on YouTube and on the internet generally.